fist stick knife gun

A Personal History of Violence

Geoffrey Canada

Beacon Press
Boston

Beacon Press
25 Beacon Street
Boston, Massachusetts 02108-2892
www.beacon.org

Beacon Press books
are published under the auspices of
the Unitarian Universalist Association of Congregations.

19   8

Composition by Wilsted & Taylor

Library of Congress Cataloging-in-Publication Data
Canada, Geoffrey.
Fist stick knife gun : a personal history of violence / Geoffrey Canada. — Rev. ed.
p. cm.
ISBN 978-0-8070-4461-2 (pbk. : alk. paper)
1. Children and violence—New York (State)—New York. 2. Violence in
children—New York (State)—New York. 3. Children—New York (State)—
New York—Social conditions. I. Title.
HQ784.V55C36   2010
303.6083'0973091732—dc22
2010030128

This book is dedicated to my mother
Mary Canada
*and to other women who
have had to do it on their own.*

Contents

•

Part III: The Best Way We Know How

Preface

•

It was a bad summer, the summer of 1993 in New York City. Late August
saw a sixteen-year-old mother accidently shot by a thirteen-year-old boy. He
was trying to shoot a sixteen-year-old boy. The young mother was trying
to save her baby, who was playing a few yards away. She was climbing a
small fence that surrounded the playground. The bullet entered her head,
killing her instantly, leaving her draped on the fence. Several days later
the police arrested two other boys, both teenagers, who were accused of
killing a thirteen-year-old girl. The girl was raped, cut several times with a
knife, then as she lay half dead and moaning, one boy stomped on her neck,
over and over. She was placed in a large box, carried to an abandoned lot,
and hours later one boy came back to set the box on fire. The girl's body,
burned beyond recognition, was discovered by firefighters who came to
put out the fire.

Then, on August 29, a ten-year-old boy was shot. Two men had another
man, their intended victim, in hand, guns out, when he broke away and ran
for his life. They managed to shoot him in his thigh, also managed to shoot
ten-year-old Luis Rivera in the head. The last the papers reported, Luis was
in very critical condition.

Preface

The summer is the worst time for the children I know. More of them are outside. Too hot and too boring to be inside. There are few jobs for the teenagers. Life is lived and lost on the streets. By the time they shot little Luis in the head in August, sixty other innocent bystanders under sixteen had been shot that year in New York City. There would be more. It really is getting worse. Too many guns, too much crack, too few jobs, so little hope.

America has long had a love affair with violence and guns. It's our history, we teach it to all of our young. The Revolution, the "taming of the West," the Civil War, the world wars, and on and on. Guns, justice, righteousness, freedom, liberty—all tied to violence. Even when we try to teach about non-violence, we have to use the Reverend Dr. Martin Luther King Jr., killed by the violent. I'm sorry, America, but once you get past the rhetoric, what we really learn is that might does make right. Poor people have just never had any might. But they want it. Oh, how they want it.

It is because most people in this country don't have to think about their personal safety every day that our society is still complacent about the violence that is engulfing our cities and towns. What if I were to tell you that we are approaching one of the most dangerous periods in our history since the Civil War? Rising unemployment, shifting economic priorities, hundreds of thousands of people growing up poor and with no chance of employment, never having held a legal job. A whole generation who serve no useful role in America now and see no hope of a future role for themselves. A new generation, the handgun generation. Growing up under the conditions of war. War as a child, war as an adolescent, war as an adult. War never ending.

Not like Vietnam, where Americans, if they survived, came home. The war today *is* home. There is not even the hope of getting out. You just survive. Day by day, hour by hour. Year after year after year.

For the handgun generation there is no post-traumatic stress syndrome because there is no "post." We need a new term to describe what happens to people who never get out from under war conditions, maybe "continuing traumatic stress syndrome." I used to read that the thing that made the Vietnamese such fierce fighters was that they had been fighting for many decades. I don't know if this is true or not, but I've watched children grow up fighting with guns, and now they're young adults. The next generation might be called the Uzi generation because of their penchant for automatic weapons. These children, armed better than the police, are growing up as violent if not more so than the handgun generation. And the gun manufacturers in their greed continue to pump more and more guns into our already saturated ghettos.

Some may think that this violence is new, but it's not. Violence has always been around, usually concentrated amongst the poor. The difference is that we never had so many guns in our inner cities. The nature of the violent act has changed from the fist, stick, and knife to the gun. But violence, I remember.

Part I

•

Codes of Conduct

Chapter One

●

The Jacket

I was probably four when I first became aware of violence. We were living in the Bronx on Cauldwell Avenue. My mother, my three brothers, and I in a small apartment. My father lived there for some small portion of that early part of my life but he was not a strong presence in our family. My mother and he were already breaking up. His drinking was becoming intolerable, his financial support sporadic at best, as he seemed incapable of keeping a job. The images from this part of my life are cloudy today, and memories of my father are neutral. He was not a bad man; he treated us well. He was just not much of a father. Even as a very young child I knew our survival depended on my mother. This didn't bother me at the time. Later the fragility of our ability to survive would have a profound impact on my brothers and me, but I was four and the world seemed fine.

My father and mother separated sometime that year. He left us, four boys, no child support, no nothing. For the next fifteen years we would go visit him every now and then. He was lost to alcohol and took on the job of superintendent of a building in Harlem. He later remarried. We barely noticed his leaving. When we visited we mostly went to see what he looked like after a few years. Whatever pressure and stress his leaving put on my mother, having to raise four boys alone, she didn't show to us. We thought everything was fine. But we were young, still living in a childhood period of innocence.

Down the block from us was a playground. It was nearby and we didn't have to cross a street to get there. We were close in age. My oldest brother, Daniel, was six, next came John, who was five, I was four, and my brother Reuben was two. Reuben and I were unable to go to the playground by ourselves because we were too young. But from time to time my two oldest brothers would go there together and play.

I remember them coming inside one afternoon having just come back from the playground. There was great excitement in the air. My mother noticed right away and asked, "Where's John's jacket?"

My brother John responded, "This boy . . . this boy he took my jacket."

Well, we all figured that was the end of that. My mother would have to go and get the jacket back. But the questioning continued. "What do you mean, he took your jacket?"

"I was playing on the sliding board and I took my jacket off and left it on the bench, and this boy he tried to take it. And I said it was my jacket, and he said he was gonna take it. And he took it. And I tried to take it back, and he pushed me and said he was gonna beat me up."

To my mind John's explanation was clear and convincing, this case was closed. I was stunned when my mother turned to my oldest brother, Daniel, and said, "And what did you do when this boy was taking your brother's jacket?"

Daniel looked shocked. What did he have to do with this? And we all recognized the edge in my mother's voice. Daniel was being accused of something and none of us knew what it was.

Daniel answered, "I didn't do nuthin'. I told Johnny not to take his jacket off. I told him."

My mother exploded. "You let somebody take your brother's jacket and you did nothing? That's your younger brother. You can't let people just take your things. You know I don't have money for another jacket. You better not ever do this again. Now you go back there and get your brother's jacket."

My mouth was hanging open. I couldn't believe it. What was my mother talking about, go back and get it? Dan and Johnny were the same size. If the boy was gonna beat up John, well, he certainly could beat up Dan. We wrestled all the time and occasionally hit one another in anger, but none of us knew how to fight. We were all equally incompetent when it came to fighting. So it made no sense to me. If my mother hadn't had that look in her eye I would have protested. Even at four years old I knew this wasn't fair. But I also knew that look in my mother's eye. A look that signified a line not to be crossed.

My brother Dan was in shock. He felt the same way I did. He tried to protest. "Ma, I can't beat that boy. It's not my jacket. I can't get it. I can't."

My mother gave him her ultimatum. "You go out there and get your brother's jacket or when you get back I'm going to give you a beating that will be ten times as bad as what that little thief could do to you. And John, you go with him. Both of you better bring that jacket back here."

The tears began to flow. Both John and Dan were crying. My mother ordered them out. Dan had this look on his face that I had seen before. A stern determination showed through the tears. For the first time I didn't want to go with my brothers to the park.

I waited a long ten minutes and then, to my surprise, John and Dan triumphantly strolled into the apartment. Dan had John's jacket in his hand.

My mother gathered us all together and told us we had to stick together. That we couldn't let people think we were afraid. That what she had done in making Dan go out and get the jacket was to let us know that she would not tolerate our becoming victims. I listened unconvinced. But I knew that in not going with Dan and John I'd missed something important. Dan was scared when he left the house. We were all scared. I knew I could never have faced up to that boy. How did Dan do it? I wanted to know everything.

"What happened? How did you do it? Did you have to fight? Did you beat him up?" I asked. Dan explained that when he went back to the playground the boy was still there, wearing John's jacket. He went up to him and demanded the jacket. The boy said no. Dan grabbed the jacket and began to take it off the boy. Dan was still crying, but the boy knew it was not from fear of him. A moment of resistance, but Dan's determination prevailed.

The boy grew scared and Dan wrestled the jacket free. He even managed a threatening "You better never bother my brother again" as the boy fled.

Dan's description of the confrontation left me with more questions. I was trying to understand why Dan was able to get the jacket. If he could get it later, why didn't he take it back the first time? How come the boy didn't fight? What scared him off? Even at four years old I knew I needed to know these things. I needed some clues on which I could build a theory of how to act. Dan's story couldn't help me much. It took many years of playing and hanging on the streets of the South Bronx before I began to put together the pieces of the theory. The only real lesson I learned from the jacket episode was if someone takes something from you, tell your mother you lost it, otherwise you might be in danger of getting your face punched in by some boy on the streets of New York City. This was a valuable bit of understanding for a four-year-old in the Bronx.

I have remembered this incident often over the course of my professional career. I have counseled so many children who've said they acted violently because their parents told them to. Parents often give instructions similar to those my mother gave my brother: fight back or I will beat you when you get home. Many times children as young as six and seven would bring weapons to school, or pick up bottles, bricks, or whatever was at hand. When asked about their violent behavior they'd often say their parents told them to "get something and bash his head in."

The children were telling the truth. In the decades I have spent counseling, teaching, and running programs for poor, inner-city children, I have seen a steady stream of parents who have given their children these instructions. The parents, inevitably single women raising children in the midst of an urban war zone, come with similar stories of children being victimized again and again. Institutions doing nothing to protect the child. The child coming home scared, scarred, looking to them for protection that they could not provide. The parents feeling as if they had no alternative. Accept it, this is a violent world, so teach them to cope by acting more violently than the others.

I tried to help these parents because I understood their anger, their desperation. They felt like I had once felt. It was 1976, the city was Boston. My daughter, Melina, was six and in the first grade; my son, Jerry, was four. I remember the shock and horror of my daughter getting off the bus (Boston was under court order to desegregate its schools and most children were bused) coming home from school crying in fear and pain. Another little girl on the bus had started bullying her and had ended up raking her face with her fingernails, leaving a set of four bloody trails down Melina's face. I was livid. My daughter knew nothing about fighting. Her beautiful face disfigured. Her sense of safety destroyed. She reported that the little girl had long nails just for fighting, and she showed me her own short nails as evidence of her defenselessness.

I did what every good parent would do. I called the school and the bus company and demanded a meeting. We met and talked. I wanted to meet the other girl's parents; no one showed up. I wanted the girl suspended. They couldn't do that; she was only seven herself. I wanted extra security on the bus; they didn't have the money. I wanted some assurance my daughter would not be attacked again; they would do their best. They did everything except give me what I wanted, a clear sense that they knew how precious my daughter was to me. That I would fight and die if necessary to protect her. That I couldn't look into her eyes again and see such fear and pain. That I was a crazy man ready to do something desperate and they needed to take that seriously.

But she wasn't *their* daughter, and most of the people I was talking with felt things like that happened every day in the Boston public schools. So I did what so many parents do across this violent nation. I sat my daughter down and told her she was never again to let any boy or girl attack her without fighting back. I had taught my children that fighting was wrong, that hitting was wrong. But like my mother before me I didn't want my daughter to be a victim. Under different circumstances I might have been able to put Melina in a safer, private school, but I was one year out of graduate school, with no money, teaching for a living.

Unlike my mother, I knew how to fight. I knew about violence. I was able to be very specific about what to do and when to do it. My daughter finished her school years with no love for violence, but she never again became a victim.

When I sit now with mothers whose children have hit someone with a bottle, or brought a knife to school, I remember how I felt about my daughter. There are few people, these parents think, who understand how scared they are for their children, not just about the incident that has brought them to me, but every day, all the time. Many of them see their child as a fawn penned in amongst lion cubs. They know that the cubs will scratch and bite, eventually even kill the fawn. They feel their job is to turn their child into a lion cub, to help that child learn to scratch and bite back.

My mother looked at her four boys that day when John had his jacket taken and made the decision that for her eldest sons the time of innocence had ended. It was time to learn about the laws of the jungle. As for me, I had heard about the lion cubs outside, but I was not allowed out by myself and so I had never run into them. I didn't know it, but my time of innocence was quickly running out.

Chapter Two

●

My New Friend

I tell people that we were the poorest welfare cheats that there ever was. A mother and four boys, and with welfare and my mother working for slave wages (that's all they paid even the most competent black women in 1958), she could barely keep a roof over our heads. We moved several times when I was small. When I was six, we moved further up in the Bronx. I was still kept under my mother's watchful eye most of the time, but occasionally I was allowed to go to the store.

I remember one day asking my mother if I could go over and over again. Finally she relented and I was given a dollar and sent one block away to the local A & P supermarket for a can of pork and beans. The boy who approached me as I paid for my purchase was maybe eight and seemed very interested in being my friend. He was a raggedy little boy with a circle on his head where no hair grew because of ringworm. He asked if we could walk back together. I was thrilled. Since moving onto this block I had met no friends, and now I couldn't believe my good fortune. He put his arm around me and said we were going to be best friends. He suggested we take a shortcut, which I quickly recognized as a longer route, but I didn't argue. He was my friend. There was an alley leading to the back of my apartment building, and it was there that he turned on me. "Give me your money," was all he said. I was in shock. The threat was more implied than stated.

The money was in my hand, some change balled up in the receipt. I couldn't move. My new friend was robbing me. He grabbed my hand and began to take the money. I watched him as if it was a movie. The thought came to me, Hit him with the can of pork and beans in the bag. He didn't know what was in there. If I hit him on the head he would be too shocked and hurt to do anything for a second or two, and I was so close to home. I looked at him. He was intent on prying my fingers loose; he wasn't even looking at me. "Hit him, hit him!" my mind screamed. But I couldn't. I couldn't hit him. He took the money and just walked away. I watched him, not knowing what to do. My mind was reeling. What had just happened? Why did the boy pick me? Why couldn't I bring myself to hit him, to fight back?

When I went back upstairs I didn't know what to do. The sixty-one cents he took from me was not a trivial amount of money to our family. I wanted to go get it back. If I told my mother, she might come with me to retrieve our money. On the other hand, I remembered what I'd learned from the incident with Dan and John and the coat. My mother might just send me out with my brothers to find the boy. I was quite convinced that this boy was different from the boy that took John's coat. He would fight. He would probably beat up all of us.

In the end I knew that it was too much money for us not to try to get it back. I told my mother what had happened. My mother and I went looking for the boy with the spot on his head, the ringworm. But he was long gone.

Later, at home, my mother warned me again about strangers. I explained that this little boy pretended to be my friend. She explained that he was just "getting my guard down" and that I had to keep my guard up all the time. I told her that I understood. I was really concerned because she had trusted me to go to the store, and losing the money might mean I couldn't go out by myself anymore. So I was completely surprised when she gave me another dollar to go back to the store to get some rice. She could tell how much my self-confidence had been shaken by being robbed. No time to "mope around the house" over one incident, get right back on the horse, she figured. I was so happy. I started looking for the boy with ringworm when I was a block away from my building. I looked at every boy. He was nowhere to be seen. All summer I looked for the boy with ringworm. In my mind he became the epitome of danger, of the "bad boys" that were outside. He became a monster. I had fantasies of smashing him with a can of pork and beans and watching him run home crying.

From time to time my mother took us to visit with her friends. We knew so few people in this part of the Bronx that my mother worried about us meeting other children. This one evening we were standing together waiting to be introduced to one of my mother's girlfriends—the four of us in a row, each sticking out his hand and saying hello—when in he marched. The boy with the ringworm. Well, the ringworm was mostly gone, actually, but you could still see the spot where the hair hadn't caught up with the rest of the hair on his head. I looked at him, thinking this would be the moment of truth. His head was down and he seemed as shy as the rest of us. He met Dan, then John. Then my turn, and . . . nothing. He didn't recognize me. Looked me in the eye, said, "Hi," and that was it.

The evening was a quiet one. My mother was off talking to her friend. I pulled my brothers aside and told them he was the ringworm boy who had robbed me. The boy seemed really eager to make friends, and he tried to break through our icy response to him. He was no monster. I felt embarrassed that I had ever let him scare me so. He was no bigger than my brothers and seemed nervous around them. After we left I told my mother about the boy. She later told her girlfriend, who ashamedly returned the sixty-one cents. I walked to the store the rest of that summer unafraid. I thought I had worked out all of the violence and fear issues in my life.

Chapter Three

•

Union Avenue

In the summer of 1959 we moved again. I was in the second grade. We were lucky to find the apartment at 1165 Union Avenue. It was the first apartment building we'd lived in that had a lot of children living on the block. Children were everywhere, playing on the sidewalks, playing in the street, sitting on cars. Everyone seemed to be laughing and running and having the time of their lives.

The apartment seemed huge to me. Two bedrooms, a living room, and a kitchen. The two bedrooms faced the street and we could look out of our third floor windows and see everything that was going on. I didn't know what a ghetto was then. Later I would learn that we lived in "the slums"; I thought we had just moved to paradise.

Paradise didn't last long. The day after our arrival my mother sent my brother Daniel to the store with ten dollars. Ten dollars was a great deal of money to us, probably one fifth of what we had to live on for the week. Dan, only nine, came back solemn and scared, and announced he'd been robbed. One of the older boys, a teenager, had probably seen Dan receive the change in the store and had followed him into our building and taken the money.

We called the police. We couldn't afford to lose ten dollars. They took their time coming and I'm sure were quite amused at this naive family, so serious about catching a petty thief in the South Bronx. This contact with the police shook my confidence in the world. Something was terribly wrong here. It was nothing they did, it was what they didn't do. They didn't take us seriously. They came because they had to come. They asked questions not because they thought the answers might help catch the thief, but because they had to do something when we were so insistent. I looked at the two white officers and realized that while their mouths were saying one thing, their manner and attitude were saying something else. We can't believe you made us walk up all these stairs for a lousy robbery of ten dollars. What's the matter with you people, don't you know where you live? Don't waste our time with this small-time crap. We'll come because we have to, but we don't have to do anything. You're on your own.

The lesson was straightforward and clear. The police didn't care. This lesson would be reinforced again and again as I grew older. It would be more than twenty years before I would call them again. Like many others trapped in the ghettos of this country, I had learned that police are not the answer when trouble comes to your door.

We never found the boy who robbed us. That afternoon when I looked out the window onto Union Avenue I couldn't believe that everyone was playing as if nothing was wrong. We had just been robbed and no one seemed to care. I was seven, and I expected that everything would come to a standstill because of our personal loss. I wanted to yell out the window to all the people on the block, "Hey, watch out! There's a robber of children out there. Be careful, it's not safe. Boys and girls, go tell your parents. Someone is robbing the children!" I didn't know it at the time, but if I had yelled that out the window some would have paused, looked at me, and kept playing; some would not have even paused. They knew what went on on Union Avenue.

* * *

14

The windows facing Union Avenue became the favorite place for my brothers and me. You could hear the street noise and see the nonstop action perfectly from this vantage point. It was not long before the other boys our age noticed that some new boys had moved in. My brother John and I were looking out the window shortly after moving on the block when we noticed some boys looking up at us. We couldn't wait to make some friends and go downstairs and play with them. We both waved. One of the boys, the biggest one, balled up his fist, placed it to his eye, pointed at us, and placed his balled-up fist to his eye again. I looked behind me, sure that he must be pointing to someone else. I pointed to myself and mouthed the words "Me? Me?" with a quizzical look. The boy repeated the gestures. The message was clear. The reception we would receive downstairs would not be a friendly one.

We quickly huddled, my brothers and I. We needed to figure this thing out. We tried my mother first. I was always the one who drew these tough assignments because I was so talkative. I mentioned, as casually as I could, "Hey, Ma, I think the boys downstairs are gonna beat us up."

She replied, "Don't be silly. You haven't done anything to them. You can't be scared to go outside and make new friends. Just be friendly, they'll play with you. It'll be just fine."

I took the bad news back to my brothers. "Ma doesn't think they're gonna fight us." They took it stoically. We were on our own and we didn't know what to do. We practiced fighting for a day or two, thinking that would help prepare us. Then my brother John went outside. We all waited to see what would happen. It was natural that John would be the first. He was one of the greatest natural athletes that I have ever seen. He was tall and thin, already taller than our older brother, Dan, and he loved sports. He lived to play ball. Any kind of ball—stickball, basketball, football—you name it, he played it better than anyone else. He found staying inside torture. He went out to take his licks.

He had to fight Paul Henry. The older boys arranged the match. There were rules. You had to be the same age, approximately the same size, and you had to fight.

* * *

On Union Avenue, failure to fight would mean that you would be set upon over and over again. Sometimes for years. Later I would see what the older boys did to Butchie.

Butchie was a "manchild," very big for his age. At thirteen he was the size of a fully grown man. Butchie was a gentle giant. He loved to play with the younger boys and was not particularly athletic. Butchie had one flaw: he would not fight. Everyone picked on him. The older teenagers (fifteen and sixteen) were really hard on him. He was forever being punched in the midsection and chest by the older boys for no reason. (It was against the rules to punch in the face unless it was a "fair fight.")

I don't know what set the older boys off, or why they picked that Saturday morning, but it was decided that Butchie had to be taught a lesson. The older boys felt that Butchie was giving the block a bad reputation. Everyone had to be taught that we didn't tolerate cowards. Suddenly two of them grabbed Butchie. Knowing that something was wrong, that this was not the rough and tumble play we sometimes engaged in, Butchie broke away. Six of the older boys took off after him. Butchie zigzagged between the parked cars, trying desperately to make it to his building and the safety of his apartment. One of the boys cut him off and, kicking and yelling, Butchie was snagged.

By the time the other five boys caught up, Butchie was screaming for his mother. We knew that his mother often drank heavily on the weekends and were not surprised when her window did not open and no one came to his aid. One of the rules of the block was that you were not allowed to cry for your mother. Whatever happened you had to "take it like a man." A vicious punch to the stomach and a snarled command, "Shut the fuck up," and Butchie became quiet and stopped struggling. The boys marched him up the block, away from his apartment. Butchie, head bowed, hands held behind his back, looked like a captured prisoner.

There were about twelve of us younger boys out that morning playing football in the street. When the action started we stopped playing and prepared to escape to our individual apartment buildings. We didn't know if the older boys were after us, too—they were sometimes unpredictable—and we nervously kept one eye on them and one on a clear avenue of escape. As they marched Butchie down the block it became apparent that we were meant to learn from what was going to happen to Butchie, that they were really doing this for us.

The older boys took Butchie and "stretched" him. This was accomplished by four boys grabbing Butchie, one on each arm, one on each leg. Then they placed him on the trunk of a car (in the early 1960s the cars were all large) and pulled with all their might until Butchie was stretched out over the back of the car. When Butchie was completely, helplessly exposed, two of the boys began to punch him in his stomach and chest. The beating was savage. Butchie's cries for help seemed only to infuriate them more. I couldn't believe that a human body could take that amount of punishment. When they finished with him, Butchie just collapsed in the fetal position and cried. The older boys walked away talking, as if nothing had happened.

To those of us who watched, the lesson was brutal and unmistakable. No matter who you fought, he could never beat you *that* bad. So it was better to fight even if you couldn't win than to end up being "stretched" for being a coward. We all fought, some with more skill and determination than others, but we all fought.

The day my brother John went out to play on the block and had to fight Paul Henry there was plenty of wild swinging and a couple of blows landed, but they did no real damage. When no one got the better of the other after six or seven minutes, the fight was broken up. John and Paul Henry were made to shake hands and became best of friends in no time.

John was free. He could go outside without fear. I was still trapped. I needed help figuring out what would happen when I went outside. John was not much help to me about how the block worked. He was proud that he could go out and play while we were still stuck in the house. I mentioned something about going downstairs and having Ma come down to watch over me and John laughed at me, called me a baby. He had changed, he had accepted the rules—no getting mothers to fight your battles. His only instructions to me were to fight back, don't let the boys your age hit you without hitting back. Within a week I decided I just couldn't take it, and I went downstairs.

The moment I went outside I began to learn about the structure of the block and its codes of conduct. Each excursion taught me more. The first thing I learned was that John, even though he was just a year older than me, was in a different category than I was. John's peers had some status on the block; my peers were considered too young to have any.

At the top of the pecking order were the young adults in their late teens (seventeen, eighteen, and nineteen). They owned the block; they were the strongest and the toughest. Many of them belonged to a gang called the Disciples. Quite a few had been arrested as part of a police crackdown on gangs in the late fifties and early sixties. Several came out of jail during my first few years on Union Avenue. They often spent large amounts of time in other areas of the Bronx, so they were really absentee rulers.

At this time there were some girls involved in gang activities as well; many of the larger male gangs had female counterparts whose members fought and intimidated other girls. On Union Avenue there was a group of older girls who demanded respect, and received it, from even the toughest boys on the block. Some of these girls were skilled fighters, and boys would say "she can fight like a boy" to indicate that a girl had mastered the more sophisticated techniques of fistfighting. Girls on Union Avenue sometimes found themselves facing the same kind of violence as did boys, but this happened less often. All in all there was less pressure on girls to fight for status, although some did; for girls to fight there usually had to be a major triggering incident.

But status was a major issue for boys on the block. The next category in the pecking order was the one we all referred to as the "older boys," fifteen and sixteen years old. They belonged to a group we sometimes called the Young Disciples, and they were the real rulers of Union Avenue. This was the group that set the rules of conduct on the block and enforced law and order. They were the ones who had stretched Butchie.

Next were boys nine, ten, and eleven, just learning the rules. While they were allowed to go into the street and play, most of them were not allowed off the block without their mother's permission. My brother John belonged to this group.

The lowest group was those children who could not leave the sidewalk, children too young to have any status at all. I belonged to this group and I hated it. The sidewalk, while it provided plenty of opportunity to play with other children, seemed to me to be the sidelines. The real action happened in the street.

There were few expectations placed on us in terms of fighting, but we were not exempt. There was very little natural animosity among us. We played punchball, tag, and "red light, green light, one-two-three." It was the older boys who caused the problems. Invariably, when the older boys were sitting on the stoop and one of them had a brother or cousin amongst us, it would be he who began the prelude to violence.

I'd been outside for more than a week and thought that I had escaped having to fight anyone because all the boys were my friends. But sure enough, Billy started in on me.

"David, can you beat Geoff?"

David looked at me, then back at Billy. "I don' know."

"What! You can't beat Geoff? I thought you was tough. You scared? I know you ain't scared. You betta not be scared."

I didn't like where this conversation was heading. David was my friend and I didn't know Billy, he was just an older boy who lived in my building. David looked at me again and this time his face changed, he looked threatening, he seemed angry.

"I ain't scared of him."

I was lost. Just ten minutes before David and I were playing, having a good time. Now he looked like I was his worst enemy. I became scared, scared of David, scared of Billy, scared of Union Avenue. I looked for help to the other boys sitting casually on the stoop. Their faces scared me more. Most of them barely noticed what was going on, the rest were looking half interested. I was most disheartened by the reaction of my brother John. Almost in a state of panic, I looked to him for help. He looked me directly in the eye, shook his head no, then barely perceptibly pointed his chin toward David as if to say, Quit stalling, you know what you have to do. Then he looked away as if this didn't concern him at all.

The other sidewalk boys were the only ones totally caught up in the drama. They knew that their day would also come, and they were trying to learn what they could about me in case they had to fight me tomorrow, or next week, or whenever.

During the time I was sizing up my situation I made a serious error. I showed on my face what was going on in my head. My fear and my confusion were obvious to anyone paying attention. This, I would later learn, was a rookie mistake and could have deadly consequences on the streets.

Billy saw my panic and called to alert the others. "Look at Geoff, he's scared. He's scared of you, David. Go kick his ass."

It was not lost on me that the questioning part of this drama was over. Billy had given David a direct command. I thought I was saved, however, because Billy had cursed. My rationale was that no big boy could use curses at a little boy. My brother would surely step in now and say, "C'mon, Billy, you can't curse at my little brother. After all he's only seven." Then he would take me upstairs and tell Ma.

When I looked at John again I saw only that his eyes urged me to act, implored me to act. There would be no rescue coming from him. What was worse, the other older boys had become interested when Billy yelled, "Kick his ass," and were now looking toward David and me. In their eyes this was just a little sport, not a real fight, but a momentary distraction that could prove to be slightly more interesting than talking about the Yankees, or the Giants, or their girlfriends. They smiled at my terror. Their smiles seemed to say, "I remember when I was like that. You'll see, it's not so bad."

Thinking on your feet is critical in the ghetto. There was so much to learn and so much of it was so important. It was my brother's reaction that clued me in. I knew John. He was a vicious tease at times, but he loved me. He would never allow me to be harmed and not help or at least go for help. He was telling me I had to go through this alone. I knew I could run upstairs, but what about tomorrow? Was I willing to become a prisoner in my apartment again? And what about how everyone was smiling at me? How was I ever going to play in the street with them if they thought I was such a baby? So I made the decision not to run but to fight.

I decided to maximize the benefits the situation afforded. I said, not quite with the conviction that I'd hoped for, "I'm not afraid of David. He can't beat me. C'mon, David, you wanna fight?"

There was only one problem—I didn't know how to fight. I hadn't seen Dan taking back John's coat, or John's fight with Paul Henry. But a funny thing happened after I challenged David. When I looked back at him, he didn't look quite so confident. He didn't look like he wanted to fight anymore. This gave me courage.

Billy taunted David, "You gonna let him talk to you like that? Go on, kick his ass."

Then Paul Henry chimed in, "Don't be scared, little Geoff. Go git him."

I was surprised. I didn't expect anyone to support me, especially not Paul Henry. But as I would learn later, most of these fights were viewed as sport by the bystanders. You rooted for the favorite or the underdog. Almost everyone had someone to root for them when they fought.

David put up his balled-up fists and said, "Come on." I didn't know how to fight, but I knew how to pretend fight. So I "put up my dukes" and stood like a boxer. We circled one another.

"Come on."

"No, *you* come on."

Luckily for me, David didn't know how to fight either. The older boys called out encouragement to us, but we didn't really know how to throw a punch. At one point we came close enough to one another for me to grab David, and we began to wrestle. I was good at this, having spent many an hour wrestling with my three brothers.

Wrestling wasn't allowed in a "real" fight, but they let us go at it a few moments before they broke us up. The older boys pronounced the fight a tie and made us shake hands and "be friends." They rubbed our heads and said, "You're all right," and then gave us some pointers on how to really fight. We both basked in the glory of their attention. The other sidewalk boys looked at us with envy. We had passed the first test. We were on our way to becoming respected members of Union Avenue.

David and I became good friends. Since we'd had a tie we didn't have to worry about any other older boys making us fight again. The rule was that if you fought an opponent, and could prove it by having witnesses, you didn't have to fight that person again at the command of the older boys. This was important, because everyone, and I mean everyone, had to prove he could beat other boys his age. Union Avenue, like most other inner-city neighborhoods, had a clear pecking order within the groups as well as between them when it came to violence. The order changed some as boys won or lost fights, but by and large the same boys remained at the top. New boys who came on the block had to be placed in the pecking order. If they had no credentials, no one to vouch for their ability, they had to fight different people on the block until it could be ascertained exactly where they fit in. If you refused to fight, you moved to the bottom of the order. If you fought and lost, your status still remained unclear until you'd won a fight. Then you'd be placed somewhere between the person you lost to and the person you beat.

The pecking order was important because it was used to resolve disputes that arose over games, or girls, or money, and also to maintain order and discipline on the block. Although we were not a gang, there were clear rules of conduct, and if you broke those rules there were clear consequences. The ranking system also prevented violence because it gave a way for boys to back down; if everybody knew you couldn't beat someone and you backed down, it was no big deal most of the time.

My "fight" with David placed me on top of the pecking order for boys on the sidewalk. I managed to get through the rest of the summer without having to fight anyone else. I had learned so much about how Union Avenue functioned that I figured I would soon know all I needed about how to survive on the block.

Chapter Four

●

"Program Busters"

As an adult I have heard many times the debate about whether violence is part of the human makeup or a learned behavior. There is no way that I can buy the theory that humans have some genetic predisposition to violence. I know better. I remember clearly the time in my life when I knew nothing of violence and how hard I worked later to learn to become capable of it. My initial belief that violence is learned has been reinforced by years of counseling and teaching children and adolescents in inner-city neighborhoods in Boston and New York.

I began teaching in Boston in 1975, right after receiving my master's degree in education. The Robert White School was a private day school for "emotionally disturbed adolescents." Really, the school was the last stop before jail or a locked psychiatric hospital for teenagers from Boston's slums. These were white students from the projects and tenements of Charlestown, East Boston, South Boston, and Dorchester. This was Boston during the beginning of busing and the start of a violent period of confrontation between blacks and whites.

Most of the students I taught had never had a black teacher before, and their racism was deeply ingrained. For me, the Robert White School was a most unusual learning experience. I had grown up as segregated as my students in terms of housing, and my first twelve years of school were spent in classrooms that were 95 percent minority.

My first real contact with white students had been Bowdoin College, a small, exclusive, overwhelmingly white college in Brunswick, Maine, where I had applied knowing only that it was a small college up north. My priorities at eighteen were to meet plenty of girls, to aid "the Movement" (remember, this was 1970, and the end of the civil rights movement, the deaths of Martin Luther King Jr. and Malcolm X, and the "long hot summers" were all a part of adolescence for black Americans my age), and, finally, to go to a good college. I was stunned when I found out that Bowdoin was (then) all male, and crushed when I found out that Brunswick had no black section and few black people living there at all. There went my fantasy of a college life filled with "working with the people" during the week and plenty of dates on the weekends. Next—because I was convinced that the only way poor children could break the cycle of poverty was through education, and because of the support of several exceptional professors who encouraged my desire to return to the inner city—I went to Harvard's Graduate School of Education, which, again, was mostly white. Both schools had confirmed my beliefs about the white world—rich kids, well educated, on their way to ruling the world. What a shock it was for me to see the poverty and ignorance in the white slums of Boston.

Most of the children at the Robert White School had been thrown out of their regular public schools, usually for acting violently. Our student body was small, about sixty, but explosive. Fights were common. Kids cursed at one another and at teachers routinely. Fear and intimidation were commonplace. It took me a while to get adjusted and to establish myself at the school, but I learned quickly that these white students were by and large just like the kids I had grown up with in the Bronx. They were poor, angry, estranged from society; they had parents who were as troubled as they were (if not more so); and most of all they were preoccupied with violence.

And, just like in the Bronx, a small number of kids set the tone. I took a long hard look at violence in this small, controlled setting. You could literally see the impact on our small society when these key actors were in school, as opposed to the days they were absent. I've subsequently called these children "program busters," because unless you can change them, they will change your whole program and you will end up with chaos.

These youngsters were characterized by extreme defiance and the open use of violence and intimidation. Their position was "I'm not scared of you. There's nothing you can do to me. Get out of my face." They were loud, aggressive, and scary young men (most were men, but not all). They had never run into an adult who could control them, who was not afraid of the obvious layer of violence that was always so close to the surface of their actions.

These "program busters" counted on the fact that teachers soon learned it was better to just let them get away with their petty harassment and intimidation. If a teacher confronted them there was likely to be a big scene, which might turn violent. Teachers avoided the stress these students created by turning a blind eye to their violent behavior. This very obvious double standard drove all the other students in the school over the edge. They knew that a couple of students were allowed to get away with stuff nobody else could. They knew there was no one to protect them if certain students threatened them or hit them. I've seen it over and over again; when children feel that adults cannot or will not protect them, they devise ways of protecting themselves. In schools or programs that allow certain children to get out of control, this has a ripple effect on other children. They start posturing, they become more violent, they become less manageable.

Within six months of my starting work at the Robert White School, its director realized that I could work with these very angry and violent young men. I began to draw the most violent students to work with. For me it wasn't that difficult once I understood who these children were and how they had grown up. I quickly understood that even the most violent of them would not have lasted more than a couple of weeks in the South Bronx. They had mastered one key component of living by violence—intimidation. But they had never learned the rest. None of them could really fight. They would beat up on the weaker children and those who were afraid. They would start fights with their peers when teachers were around who had to break up the fight. But they hadn't had the kind of fights that separate those with a lot of mouth from those who know the "science" of violence.

I used this knowledge to my advantage when I became the director of the school in 1977, to control the violence and the residual impact that it had on the rest of the student body. It was not an easy process. Teachers had to be retrained, and everyone had to know that it took time to change the culture of a school. But in the end it happened.

There were many times when one or two students could have a negative impact on the whole school, and I knew that finding the solution to controlling their behavior was the key to running a safe program.

At one point, for example, there were these two boys who hated one another. Whenever both of them were in school at the same time there was trouble, sometimes a fight. This went on and on for weeks. I noticed an interesting pattern. The fights always occurred when staff were around. Both boys came to school and left at approximately the same time. Because of the way the school was situated there was plenty of opportunity for a real "settle the score" fight before or after school. In the Bronx, fighting in front of teachers was amateurish. The real fights happened after school. These were both big boys and my staff was getting real beat up breaking up the fights, without any resolution to the problem. One day I was summoned out of my office to help break up a fight between these two. I asked that they be brought to my office.

Seven of us ended up in my relatively small office—the two boys, four teachers (two holding each boy), and myself. I asked the staff to leave. They looked at me, more than a little puzzled because they were actively restraining the boys, who were struggling to get at each other. I explained that I was going to let them fight right after I spent a couple of minutes with them, but there could be no fighting in my office.

My conversation with them went like this: "Now, now. Don't worry, fellas, you're gonna get your chance to settle this once and for all, and I know how tough you both are and how wild this fight is going to be, so I don't want my office messed up. OK?"

Everyone was looking at me as if I had lost my mind. The teachers and the students knew I had a strict no-violence code at the school. Anyone engaging in violence for any reason was to be suspended, period. While parent conferences, home visits, and counseling were all part of our violence reduction program, our first rule was no fighting for any reason. The teachers let the boys go, but they refused to leave. They didn't know where I was heading.

I continued. "Now you two really want to fight—right?" They both nodded their heads yes. "Well, you're gonna get your opportunity, I promise. In fact, I *insist* that you beat the hell out of one another until someone comes out the winner. But not in my office, all right? I just want to spend a few minutes with you first. All right?" Both young men agreed. They knew I was trying some kind of reverse psychology junk, but they knew they were too smart for that crap.

I went on. "Listen, I've had a few fights in my time. Sometimes you just have to do it. But this is nonsense. You two have been trying to fight for weeks, but you keep doing it in school. I'm beginning to think you really don't want to fight. That you're hiding behind the fact that you know we're gonna break it up."

They both began to talk at once, trying to convince me how desperately they needed to fight. I interrupted them. "Now, now, fellas. I'm going to help you out. Right across the street they have a construction site and there's a hole in the fence. No one can see you if you go into that deserted courtyard. Come here. Let me show you."

They both came to look out my window into the empty site across the street. They knew this was heading in a direction that they didn't like. They weren't as sure I was bluffing as they'd been before.

I went on. "So the important thing is for one of you to go in first. Don't look around or do anything suspicious, just step right through the hole. Then two minutes later the next one does the same thing. That way no one will call the police and you can have as much time as you need. All right, go ahead. The two of you can go in there and punch, and kick, and bite, and wrestle, and fart, and scream, and no one's gonna break you up. Wow, I wish I could be there. I know it's gonna be great! You can come back to school when you're done, or take the rest of the day off if you have to. Okay, you can go." And I stood up.

The boys stayed seated. They were in shock. They knew I really meant it. They'd never considered how a fight ends when there's no one to break it up. It didn't sound pretty. They just sat there.

I turned on them with a vengeance. "Don't want to go, huh? Well, that's it. Take it or leave it. No more fighting in school. Next time you want to fight you know the place. Just look at one another and say, 'Let's do it,' and walk out of school and do it. Now you can go back to class, or to the construction site."

Of course they went back to class. I had learned early in my life that few people want to have a real fistfight. It hurts to really fight. These two wanted all of the glory without any of the pain and sacrifice. Ha! Wouldn't have lasted a week in the South Bronx. Sooner or later the pain came to one and all.

My actions that day at the Robert White School were not based on snap judgment. I had studied my students, and I saw that many of them displayed the characteristics of the children I had grown up with in the Bronx, of the child I had been. Violence is a learned response; I know this from my earliest education on the street.

Chapter Five

•

P.S. 99

Schools in America are dangerous places. All the research shows that a significant number of high school students carry guns. Hundreds of thousands more come to school with other weapons. Schools often serve as gladiator societies for poor urban children. Intimidation, threats, and outright fights go on in classrooms, hallways, cafeterias, and schoolyards. Many children quickly learn that the teacher or principal might provide a sense of order when he or she is standing in front of you, but no one can really protect you in school except your fists and your friends.

After a spate of shootings in New York City schools, metal detectors were installed. The program was instituted in 1988 and began in sixteen high schools where the highest number of weapons were being confiscated. School security staff made unannounced sweeps using hand-held metal detectors. The program cost $300,000 per school, and by 1993 a total of forty-one schools were using detectors. By 2009, the New York Civil Liberties Union was estimating that at least 99,000 students were walking through metal detectors every school day, and that number will likely keep rising. It strikes me that while metal detectors may prevent a few guns from coming into the school, they have no real impact on the children's sense of safety. Children simply get the message "If you're going to shoot someone, it will not be in school. You must shoot them coming to school, or going home from school, but not in the school building." And this is one of the main problems with too many of our schools. Children understand that the adults who control the school are powerless to protect them. School is too often the child's learning ground about the impotence of adult authority when it comes to violence.

Public School 99 was like most elementary schools in poor communities in New York City. The school was mostly black, with Latinos making up the next largest group and then a few white students whose parents had not yet managed to flee the crumbling tenements of the South Bronx. It was there that my continuing education about survival was broadened. On Union Avenue I had begun to understand how violence worked. I believed mine was the toughest block in all of the Bronx. What I failed to understand was that Union Avenue was not much different from any of the twenty or so blocks that supplied the children who attended P.S. 99. And those twenty blocks were not much different from any others in the South Bronx. On each block there were children fighting for status, fighting for rank, fighting for respect. Then all of those children were dumped together into the schools. The old ranking order on your block meant nothing once you came in contact with children from other blocks. Fights were inevitable and often brutal.

It was at P.S. 99 that I began to appreciate what the older boys had done for me that summer. They understood that Union Avenue was really a haven for us. Even though we fought, cursed, and otherwise abused one another, basically we lived in relative safety. Once you set foot off the block you were in enemy territory. Whether you could travel without being set upon often had to do with the reputation of the block you lived on. Children from Union Avenue were considered tough, we were known to fight back, and that was a reputation we could use to our advantage. It was the job of the older boys to "make us tough" so we wouldn't become victims once we left the block.

I was dismayed to learn that you had to get a "reputation" at school the same way you did on the block. Everyone on the block or in the school who had earned the right to have one of the tougher boys say about him, "Naw, man, don't mess with him, he's all right" had had to fight for it. The difference was that you had so much more to lose when you fought in school. On the block, losing a fight might drop you down one or two people in the pecking order; in school losing a fight could drop you down twenty or thirty. People who had never bothered you before would begin to harass you and you'd have to fight over and over again to reestablish your reputation.

Fights were fairly common and they drew big crowds. Typically, before school was over for the day we would hear there was going to be a fight. The news traveled on an underground system designed to keep teachers unaware. It was not unusual for fifty to a hundred kids to be waiting at three o'clock for the combatants to come out of school. Many times one child wanted to settle the score with another who didn't even know he or she was being targeted for a fight; some boy or girl had told the teacher on the wrong person and now was going to have to pay for it outside. I will never forget the faces of these unsuspecting souls when they walked out of school to go home, only to find seventy or eighty screaming children surrounding them, and their antagonist in their face. Escape was impossible as children pressed tight in a circle to be able to see every gory detail.

Like on the block, there were rules to these schoolyard battles. There were times you could be rescued from the situation if a friend challenged the other boy or girl and stood to take your place. But this convention added danger to any fight situation because just as your friend could volunteer to fight for you, someone else might volunteer to fight for the other person. You could end up with two new people fighting who really had nothing to fight about. There was also the possibility that the crowd would get into it. One of the most common responses from the spectators was "Why don't you pick on somebody your own size?" The rules of Union Avenue prevailed at P.S. 99: you had to fight people your own age who were approximately your size. Sometimes total strangers would intervene and break up the fight if it was judged to be unfair. But most times you had to fight or live with public ridicule.

It was at P.S. 99 that I learned that Union Avenue was not the toughest block in the Bronx. There were boys who came from blocks where mayhem and chaos ruled. These boys were like hungry sharks in a feeding frenzy. Tough street fighters, they were unafraid and moved through our ranks leaving children punched, slapped, cursed, pushed, threatened, and crying. We all learned to play at lunchtime with one eye always alert for their approach. The idea was to see them coming; then you could walk away and try to get lost in the crowd of other children before one of them called you to "come here." It was an art form to saunter away without looking as if you were trying to avoid anything. If they saw you trying to escape they would command you to come to them, and none dared to refuse a direct command.

The school was ruled from the top by two boys named Tyronne and Anthony, who were said to be twins, although no one seemed to know for sure. They were fairly benevolent rulers, as they tended to leave most of us younger boys alone. Directly under the twins was a group of mean, hardened little boys. They would use their association with Tyronne and Anthony to bully anyone who might stand up to them otherwise. The fifth- and sixth-grade boys of Union Avenue who went to P.S. 99 would not challenge the twins, but they constantly tangled with that other group as they tried to keep a clear passage home for all Union Avenue kids.

Getting home safely from school was a daily struggle. There seemed always to be a fight after school. Many times you wouldn't know who the group of boys was waiting for until someone called your name as you tried to go by. A lot was at stake if you were called out. The big issue among the boys was whether or not you had "heart." Having heart meant that you were unafraid, that you would fight even if you couldn't beat the other boy. In many ways those of us on Union Avenue were a certain type of warrior class in the Bronx. We disdained bullies and were not known to bully others, but we were known as boys who had heart. The block had an identity and that identity was strengthened or weakened each time one of us had to square off after school.

The scenarios were much the same. From the crowd waiting in the schoolyard someone would call your name: "Hey, Geoff."

"Yeah, what you want, man?"

"I heard you said you could kick my ass."

"Naw, man, I didn't say that."

"Flopper said you said that you would whup my ass."

"I didn't say shit to Flopper."

"So?"

"So what?"

"So you wanna fight me or you scared?"

"I ain't scared of you, but I didn't say nothing to Flopper."

That was as far as you could go. If you became more conciliatory than that, people in the crowd would think you had no heart. If there had been a true misunderstanding and your denial was accepted you would probably get a warning and everything would be over (maybe tomorrow you'd be waiting for Flopper to fight him for lying on you). But if it was a setup and the boy just wanted an excuse to fight you, there was no use "copping a plea," as we used to say. Better to show you were more than willing to fight, to try to shake your antagonist's confidence. This sent a message to everyone in the crowd that you "weren't gonna take no shit off no one."

Once you reached that crucial point after school when there was no turning back, having someone from the block there to "watch your back" was essential. Other boys might push you off balance, or pull you off an opponent you had on the ground, or jump in if you had no one to keep an eye on the crowd while you fought. This was another reason why it was critical for the boys of Union Avenue to be able to fight and to have heart—we had to watch one another's backs.

The years I spent at P.S. 99 continued my development in learning to read and write, and also in learning to curse, intimidate, and fight. I was a fast learner both inside the classroom and out. By the time I reached the sixth grade it was recognized by all the tough boys in school that not only would I fight but I knew *how* to fight. This was particularly important for me because I was in class 6-1, the "smartest" class in the school. Many boys associated being a good student with not being able to fight, and by and large this was true. I quickly understood this liability. I kept my rich school life and my love of books to myself. While others might know I was in a "smart" class, they also knew that I didn't act like it and that I had won more than my share of fights after school. Anyone who "messed" with me knew that they would get a "hard way to go," meaning they would not make their reputation off of me, they would get no quick and easy victory in either a verbal confrontation or a physical one.

By the time I was in the sixth grade, Tyronne and Anthony were in junior high school. My brothers John and Dan were also in junior high, as were many of the other boys their age who lived on Union Avenue. I remember asking one day about whether Tyronne and Anthony, still legends at P.S. 99, were also running their new school. "Man, they ain't running shit," I was told. "They got some real bad dudes in junior high, wait and see." I remember being depressed and scared at the same time. I had worked so hard to get my own reputation at P.S. 99, and now I was being told I would have to start all over again at the bottom once I got to junior high. I remember thinking, "If it gets much tougher than this, where does it end?"

Chapter Six

•

Conditioning

Rules like the ones surrounding our behavior on Union Avenue and at P.S. 99 by and large still exist today in the ghettos across this country. If you wonder how a fourteen-year-old can shoot another child his own age in the head, or how boys can do "drive-by shootings" and then go home to dinner, you need to know you don't get there in a day, or week, or month. It takes years of preparation to be willing to commit murder, to be willing to kill or die for a corner, a color, or a leather jacket. Many of the children of America are conditioned early to kill and, more frighteningly, to die for what to an outsider might seem a trivial cause. The codes of conduct on the streets of our slums have always been hard, cold, and unforgiving. But with the influx of hundreds of thousands of handguns, you have a new brand of gunslinger among the young. Countless young people today are more dangerous than Jesse James or Billy the Kid ever were. Indeed, the Wild West was never as wild as many communities in Chicago, Los Angeles, New York, Boston (and on and on) are today. And, just as important, there's no Wyatt Earp—no one person or one program powerful enough—coming to town to clean up the mess.

It's handguns that make living in the inner city so lethal today. People have been armed and violent for a long time, but the weapon of choice used to be a bottle or a knife: the explosion of killing we see today is based on decades of ignoring the issue of violence in our inner cities. Every indicator I see suggests that it's going to get worse. How much worse? I don't think we understand the potential of how bad it can get.

A crucial part of the problem is that there are so few natural checks on killing today. This might sound strange, but while killing another person is not natural, it's not that difficult to learn. No, I've never killed anyone. But for those of you who think killing is somehow impossible to imagine, just look around the world. Wars abound—intentional starvation, the killing of civilians, women, and children—and these atrocities are sometimes committed by farmers, laborers, and other ordinary people. Even in this country the military can take an eighteen-year-old boy and turn him into a killer in a matter of months. People can be *taught* to kill. And children growing up under the conditions of war that we find in many poor communities today learn to think about death and killing as a matter of survival. And of course there are always those who are willing to teach children how to kill, and how to die. These are usually the real role models in our inner cities, older boys or girls who teach the codes of conduct and enforce the rules of order.

When I was growing up in the South Bronx there were some natural checks on violent behavior. Most violence on the block was done with the fists in what we called a "fair one": two people fought until one was too hurt to continue or quit in defeat. There were people around to ensure the dispute was settled according to the rules. No "dirty" fighting was allowed, no kicking or biting, no weapons. If someone violated the rules he might be attacked or ostracized by the group. Violence against others who did not live on the block was not subject to the same rules—in these situations you could do whatever you liked—but even so, because none of us had guns, knife fighting was usually the most extreme form these encounters took. Anyone who has ever fought with a weapon like a knife or a bottle knows there is no glamour in it. These fights are messy and dangerous, even deadly. The use of weapons usually occurred only in someone else's territory.

The first rules I learned on Union Avenue stayed with me for all of my youth. They were simple and straightforward: Don't cry. Don't act afraid. Don't tell your mother. Take it like a man. Don't let no one take your manhood. My teachers were the typical instructors on blocks like Union Avenue—the adolescents we all looked up to.

It would have been only natural for me to try to emulate the boys who were two or three years older than I was, but I saw that they were still in the learning stage themselves. The group I sought out was the boys who were seven and eight years older, the group that dominated our block. We all looked up to them. They were both caring and offhandedly cruel toward us. We lived for their praise and cringed at the slightest sign of dissatisfaction. They considered us their charges to raise on the block, and our lessons were sometimes taught by the group and sometimes by individuals.

These boys were by and large just like others growing up in America's urban ghettos. They worked when they could, some struggled with school, only one had gone to college (and that was on a basketball scholarship). They hung out on the corners and stoops of the tenements and passed on the codes of conduct to those younger than themselves. This was a time before crack, so there was no money to be made hanging on the corner selling drugs. These boys were broke, with hopes and dreams but few opportunities. They took pride in what they had—"heart" and a fierce loyalty to one another and to the block. They had no clear leader, but two of them made up the center of the group, Mike and Junior. They were the best athletes, both could fight well, and they were respected on and off the block. They seemed to have conquered the fear and the anxiety of living in the ghetto, and I, like all the other boys, admired them and wanted their friendship and their protection.

But their friendship was basically unachievable for those of us who were so much younger. What we got were some brief moments to sit with them or stand near them. Maybe they would let one of us play on their side in a stickball game if they were desperate for another player. But more than likely we would be told to "get lost" when they saw us hanging around, or simply be looked at as if we had lost our minds or something when they wanted us to leave. If you were smart you left immediately. Those who did not were run off with curses, ridicule, sometimes a smack upside the head. We learned to read them like a thermometer; we knew when we could stay and when we had to leave. I was able to break into this group of older boys only because of my relationship with Mike.

If I have accomplished anything with my life, Mike is directly responsible. He rescued me when I was a small, helpless boy, confused and scared in the South Bronx. Try as I might, I just couldn't understand the codes of conduct on Union Avenue. In fact, when I thought about the rules of the block it reminded me of looking into my older brother's math book—familiar numbers strung together in strange ways, weird signs never seen before. I realized that if you started at the beginning of the book and had the help of a good teacher you might eventually understand what those numbers and signs meant. But on the street the price for not knowing or not responding correctly was more painful than a failing grade. And one of the first things I realized was that most of the boys my age were as uninformed as I was. They learned mostly by trial and error. The older boys often talked in absolutes when they tried to pass on useful information: "Don't ever take no shit from nobody. Anybody fuck with you, bust their ass!" We would all solemnly nod our heads like we understood. But I would be thinking, "How can he say that? Everybody takes shit from somebody. We all take shit from the older guys every day."

I once tried to question the older boys, to get more clarity on what they were trying to teach us. "Well, suppose you can't beat the kid, then what?"

The response was pure Union Avenue. First the mocking repeat of the question in a whining, high-pitched voice: "'Well, suppose you can't *beat* the kid?' Wassa matta, nigger? You scared? You sound like a little bitch. 'Well, suppose you can't *beat* the kid?' You scared of everybody bigga than you. Alan's bigga than you, you scared of him?"

Well, I knew where this was leading. Next thing you know Alan and I would be in the street fighting to the cheers of the kids on the block, all over nothing. My response was to sit down on the curb, head down, trying to become invisible, praying for a distraction or any other salvation. Try not to cry. Please, God, don't let me cry. I learned today's lesson. Shut up. Just keep quiet.

I became friends with Mike because I loved the mornings on Union Avenue. Early in the morning Union Avenue was a peaceful place. You could walk up and down the block without the usual concern about who might tease you, or laugh at the fact that your clothes were cheap or you didn't have money for a haircut. Mike also liked to get up early. He lived on his own, in a basement apartment that we called "the cut."

Mike's mother was unable or unwilling to care for him, leaving him alone to raise himself the best way he could. Mike was everything I wanted to be—handsome, athletic, tough, and, most important to me, he was smart. He read books. And he was proud of it. With Mike I could be myself. He knew I was in the top class at P.S. 99. He knew I read adult novels in the fifth grade. And on weekend and summer mornings we talked about all kinds of subjects.

It was Mike I turned to for help in understanding Union Avenue. He was the one who told me about heart, about gaining respect, about when to fight and how. Most of all Mike was my protector. It wasn't that he fought my battles. He didn't. But when I was with him I was safe, no one would bother me. And as my friendship with Mike became known to others, the zone of safety he created for me was respected by people on and off the block. The word got out quickly: "Don't mess with him, he's Mike's boy." For me, a small boy in a mean ghetto, no father, no adult male to teach me or protect me, Mike was like a knight in shining armor.

The one thing you could count on in the South Bronx, though, was that any real friendship you established would be tested time and time again. You just never knew where or what the test might be.

Mike and I established a Saturday ritual. I would go to the cut and wake him up, we would get some breakfast from a local greasy spoon, and then go shoot some baskets at the local park. Mike was intent on teaching me how to play basketball and made sure I got some practice in before the real players came on the court later in the afternoon.

Well, this one morning when I was eleven, I went to the cut, woke up Mike, grabbed the ball, and went outside to wait for him. I was shooting the ball up against a parking sign. I missed the sign and hit a new car.

Now, on our block men were always yelling at us to quit leaning on their cars and new cars were fairly rare. We knew most everybody on the block and they all knew the codes of conduct. Yelling and threatening us for sitting or leaning on a car was perfectly legitimate, but that's as far as an owner could go. We, on the other hand, had to get off the car immediately when asked and act sufficiently intimidated. It wasn't lost on us that when the older boys were on the same car, there were no threats, no yelling, but even the older boys had to respect men. (Like new cars, they were fairly rare on Union Avenue.)

A man I had never seen before was coming down the block. He saw the basketball bouncing off his new car and came storming up to me. "Give me that fucking ball!" I looked up, shocked. The menace in his voice and posture were clearly evident to me. I was scared but I had to protest. This was Mike's ball, and we all knew that you didn't let anyone take anything away from you that belonged to the older boys, especially Mike. I knew what I had to do, play the little-boy role and explain about the ball.

"Mister, this ain't my ball. This ball belongs to a boy named Mike . . ." I never got to finish the sentence. In two steps he was right on top of me, and I could tell he was trying to decide whether my impertinence demanded a slap. I cringed. He snatched the ball from my hands.

"I don't care whose fucking ball this is, it's mine now." It was final. The decision had been made.

The thing about the South Bronx was that you never could relax. Anything might happen at any given time. Here it was, eight o'clock on a beautiful, sunny summer morning, and my world was turned upside down. I was in a panic. Mike had told me about letting people push you around, and I had been doing a pretty good job of putting an end to people doing that to me. But what was I supposed to do about this huge man? Did Mike expect me to fight *him*? I couldn't. I was scared, and with my fear came an old companion—shame. I began to beg the man as the tears rolled down my face. "Please, mister, give me the ball. It ain't my ball. I'm gonna get in trouble. That's Mike's ball."

The man ignored me. He put the ball in his trunk, took out a rag, and began wiping off his car. I prayed he would drive off. Just leave with the ball, I'll tell Mike what happened and deal with the consequences. My prayers were not answered. Just then I saw Mike and his best friend, Junior, coming down the block toward me. I looked at the man. He was much bigger than Mike or Junior. I didn't like their odds.

It was Mike who spoke first. He saw my tears and with true concern asked me what was wrong. I told him that the man took his ball, my shame hot on my face. Mike didn't understand. He asked which way the man had gone. I explained that the man was right there, only five feet away, wiping down his car. Mike asked why he'd taken the ball and I told him I'd accidentally hit the car.

Mike laughed. Clearly this was just a misunderstanding. He approached the man and said calmly, "Excuse me, but you have my ball." The man turned, looked Mike up and down, and said, "That's *my* ball now, and that's it."

Mike did something I would later see him do many times whenever a situation was getting out of control. He became calm and clear. He said, "Well, maybe you didn't understand me, but that's my ball, not the kid's. Mine."

This should have been all the man needed to understand that he faced a new situation. According to the codes of conduct, no man could let another man take his property, period. If you let that happen you might as well never come back on the block, for you would get no respect from anyone ever again. So Mike was letting the man know that even though he might have thought he was taking a ball from a kid, he was really taking it from another man, one who would fight to the death to defend his property. The man could give back the ball with no loss of face. But he was not from our block and he apparently didn't know the codes of conduct on the streets of the South Bronx.

"I don't give a fuck whose ball this was, it's mine now," he said. Junior moved first. He shifted over to the man's right just enough so that the man couldn't watch him and Mike at the same time. Mike took a step to the man's left. He spoke with unmistakable conviction.

"Listen, if you don't give me my ball, I'm gonna kick your fucking ass right now all up and down this block." He took a step toward the man. Junior shifted just enough to get in a good shot. The man realized that he'd completely underestimated who he was dealing with. There was no doubt that a vicious fight was about to ensue, and the two young men he faced were not only unafraid but acting in concert in a way that conveyed that this was not the first time they had done this.

The man pulled out his car keys and took a step toward the trunk of his car. We all knew that some men carried their guns in their trunk. Things were quickly getting out of hand.

Mike's hand went into his jacket pocket, and we could all hear the click of the knife locking as he opened it quickly and efficiently with one hand. Junior put his hand inside his jacket at his neck, where I knew he often wore a chain with a combination lock on it, a dangerous weapon. Both of them stepped toward the man. If he thought he was going to scare them off he was mistaken. This was their block. They couldn't run.

I realized that this was decision time. No turning back now. Some of the swagger had gone from the man's demeanor. The trunk opened. Everyone tensed, ready for action. "Where's that jack?" he said aloud as he pulled it from the car. The situation was defused. Mike said, "Yo, man. The ball."

"All right, here it is. I'll give it to you this time," the man said, trying to save some face.

"Yeah, I'll bet you will," Mike said, unwilling to let the man off scot-free after he'd precipitated an unnecessary crisis. The ball in hand, Mike gave it back to me and we began to walk to the park.

Next came what I found the most baffling part of living on Union Avenue. Nothing. I mean *nothing*. I was filled with adrenaline, questions, fear— the emotional reservoir of my mind was overflowing. But from Mike and Junior, nothing. I tried to engage them in conversation about the incident. "He was an asshole. Forget it." That was all that was said. That morning I couldn't concentrate on shooting baskets. I kept looking at Mike. He'd been willing to risk his life for a basketball. Well, not for the ball itself, but for the principle behind Union Avenue's idea of being a man. Then afterwards he acted as if it was no big deal. How could he keep his emotions so under control? How could he switch from being ready to fight to the death to making small talk about the upcoming stickball game, all within thirty seconds?

I knew that what I had just witnessed was important. Because of the unpredictability of life in the South Bronx, you had to learn how to dominate your emotions. You couldn't dwell on issues that caused fear or anger. Things happened, you acted, you moved on. If you didn't learn how to do this you might never make it out of the Bronx alive. Or if you lived you would become a slave to your emotions, ping-ponging from one to the next. The fear, the doubt, the anger, would crowd your mind until there would be no room for any of the good things—love, friendship, laughter.

Over the years I would see many people who had literally gone mad trying to survive the unpredictability and constant pressures of the Bronx. When I was growing up we used to say someone had "lost it" to explain behaviors that were due to poor mental health. What we meant was that when a person did some outrageous act that was totally out of character, he or she had "lost their mind." One day this boy Randall lost it and chased a boy we used to call B.J. down the block with a machete. Randall was such a quiet guy, never caused any trouble. B.J. said they'd just been joking around and the next thing he knew he was running for his life. Randall later seemed fine, but we never fully trusted him again.

My life in the Bronx would be a constant struggle to do what had to be done while keeping my emotions under control. Emotions got in the way of acting, and the ability to act when you had to was crucial in maintaining some control over your environment.

Learning the process of separating fear from action took years. Mike was the teacher, I the student. In a world of violence that escalated in frequency and intensity with each year he grew older, every boy needed someone to help him figure out how and when to act. Most young people did not have the advantage I did of a teacher who'd lived long enough to know that there are no absolutes, who was tough but patient. There is nothing as dangerous as advice from a thirteen-year-old on how to handle a violent confrontation. Because I hung out with Mike I learned my lessons from some of the masters, but there was a price to pay.

Chapter Seven

●

Shamming

My first inkling that even though I was making progress in learning the codes of conduct in the Bronx there were still some quantum leaps I had to make came one evening on Union Avenue. There were only a few of us left hanging out that night by what we called the factory, a small warehouse of one kind or another. None of us knew what they did in the building because during all my years living on Union Avenue I never knew of anyone from our neighborhood hired to work there. Occasionally the metal door of the factory would open and we could see men loading metal drums onto a truck. The truck would leave, the door would come sliding down, and that would be that.

On this particular summer night there were a few older teenagers hanging with those of us who were in junior high school. The gunshots happened in rapid succession. I didn't even know what they were. One of the older boys yelled, "They're shooting!" and everyone started running. I began to run, too. My building was only fifty yards away, but the safety of the hallway had never seemed so far. Then, to my surprise, several of the other boys ran past their own buildings and headed toward Home Street, which ran perpendicular to Union Avenue.

"Over there, that's where it came from," one of them called out, and everyone headed down Home Street in the direction he pointed. I stopped. Here I thought I was running away from the gunshots and we were intentionally running toward them.

I sat on my stoop with my head ringing. I had learned how to hone my reflexes so that I could dodge rocks, punches, and bottles—but a bullet? I had learned how to jump fences, knew the dark alleys like the back of my hand and could run through them at full speed. I knew how to break a bottle on the curb to create a nasty weapon for stabbing or cutting, how to pop an antenna off a car and swing it so it would slice through flesh like a hot knife through butter. But you couldn't see a bullet. Running toward gunshots was like playing Russian roulette. Why was I the only one who stopped?

After a few minutes the others came back disappointed that they hadn't seen any gunplay. If any of them were worried about getting shot it wasn't apparent. They spent the next hour talking about what had happened even though no one really had a clue. Guns were rarely used to settle disputes during the mid-sixties and none of us owned one. Most of us had never seen a gun up close. Still, my peers could not help wanting to see what a gun could do, and they wanted to see it up close. We all knew that a gun was the ultimate weapon. Little did we know that one day guns would forever change the codes of conduct that we worked so hard to learn and live up to.

In the meantime I spent a significant amount of my time learning how to fight unarmed. There were plenty of "sham" fights, where two people were paired off to box each other with bare knuckles. In these fights you were not allowed to punch to the face, but they were an important step in our learning process at the age of eleven or twelve. You often got hurt when an opponent landed a punch solidly in your stomach or solar plexus. When you were overmatched with a stronger and more skilled opponent, even punches to the chest or ribs could drop you. The idea was to learn how to dish it out and how to take it. Crying wasn't allowed, but tears of pain or rage were tolerated. Slap boxing was another form our training took. This differed from "shamming" in that the face and head were the primary target. And just as the name implies, you had to hit with an open hand. These mock battles taught much-needed skills: how to move your head so that you presented a more difficult target, how to keep your hands up, and how to keep your eyes open even when someone was trying to "smack the hell out ya."

These exercises toughened us, prepared us for the real thing. In fighting, just like in subjects taught in school, there were those few who excelled, many who struggled but eventually learned enough to get by, and those who just couldn't get the hang of it. Most of us knew very little at first about the science of fighting; we mostly just did a poor parody of what we saw the older boys doing. And this was sufficient as long as you didn't meet up with someone who really knew what he was doing. I was a fairly good actor, and to the untrained eye I looked like I really knew how to fight.

It was Mike who showed me I didn't. One day, in front of a group of us Mike said, "Come here, Geoff, put up your hands." I was puzzled. "Put up your hands" was a command used when you were challenging someone, or when you were going to make an example of him. I knew Mike wasn't challenging me. There was no contest there. Eight years older, bigger, tougher—he would kill me. Which meant I was going to "get a lesson." I was not pleased. In fact I was terrified. I knew about the lessons the older boys taught. We all did. We'd all witnessed the lesson Kevin got.

Even though Kevin was the same age as Mike, Junior, and the other older boys, he seemed far more happy-go-lucky. No coward, Kevin, yet he was only a fairly decent fighter, not one who seemed eager to fight. This particular evening started like any other, the older guys sitting around drinking beer, talking trash. This night they didn't run us off, which was always a two-edged sword. We got to listen to them and learn from their experiences, but you never could tell when they might turn on one of us and we'd become the butt of their jokes or, worse, be hit or punched for saying something that was fine to say yesterday but offended them today.

Richard had the floor. He was a couple of years older than Mike and Junior and he was lecturing on having heart and on the need to keep your skills sharp. He was detailing different deficiencies in form or approach that some of the older boys had in their fighting styles. He called a few of them out to slap box and would stop in the middle of the match to correct the position of someone's hands or comment on his footwork. It was at these times that many of us knew we were dancing on a razor's edge. Richard or anyone else might just call us out, and if you didn't show the proper amount of courage and skill a serious beating at the hands of any one of the older boys was a certainty. So when the lessons were going on you couldn't draw any attention to yourself. If you tried to leave you would be ordered back and more than likely made to fight the next match. These sessions were looked on as school. Attendance was mandatory.

Kevin, who was overweight and only a fair athlete, tried to talk his way out of the match. "Naw, man. Naw. I don't feel like it." Richard was having none of it. "C'mon, nigger, get your fat ass out here." When Kevin resisted again it was made clear by Richard and the other older boys that Kevin's skills were just not up to par. He was too soft. He needed a lesson. I leaned against the wall like the others my age. Here it was, just another night, no one on the block but us, and what had looked like fun and games was suddenly turning more serious. Kevin was scared. He was trying to hide it but we could all see it. His friends, Junior, Mike, and the others, not only didn't help him, they began to ride Kevin themselves. There was no support for nonviolence on Union Avenue.

Finally, when it became clear that he was going to *have* to slap box with Richard, Kevin half-heartedly went into the street and put his hands up. His mistake was that he thought if he acted passively Richard would take it easy on him. A major error. Kevin began pawing at Richard, not really trying to connect. Richard's first smack to Kevin's face could be heard all the way up the block. A crowd began to form. Even as Kevin's head snapped back with the force of the blow, Richard hit him again. "Come on, nigger, fight back. Fight back or I'm gonna kick your ass," Richard said as he smacked Kevin over and over again.

Kevin began to get mad. Clumsily he threw blows at Richard, who easily ducked under them only to smack Kevin again. The blows to his face made Kevin's eyes tear. He was absorbing tremendous punishment. Try as he might, Kevin couldn't hit Richard. The others began to cheer Kevin on. They knew that if he quit he would be banned from the group. Taking a whipping was part of the price you sometimes had to pay to belong, but quitting was never allowed. No one trusted someone who couldn't take punishment, and no one trusted a quitter.

Finally the others intervened. Kevin had had enough. He had proved he could take it. Richard was just being cruel now. So they said, "Enough." Richard stopped, gave Kevin a few pointers which we all listened to, and everybody began to drink and laugh at Kevin. No false sympathy. If you wanted to hang out you had to be competent in battle. Kevin had a long way to go. But at least he'd shown he had heart.

Now that Mike was calling me out I was transfixed thinking about that night. I couldn't believe it. Mike and I were friends. What had I done? The kids my age looked at me and dropped their eyes when I looked back. A few of them smiled as if to say, You gonna get your ass kicked and better you than me. I knew I couldn't "cop a plea" and ask Mike to let me be, it didn't work like that. It would just enrage him and I would get an even worse beating. So I put up my hands and set my face to try to mask my fear.

It was a pretty brutal affair. The tears came down my cheeks with the first slap. I fought back gamely even if to no avail. After it was over Mike told me I "couldn't box worth shit." Those words stung me more than all the slaps to the face. When Junior pulled me over, though, and said, "Don't worry. You did OK. You got heart. I didn't know you had heart," I realized that even though I had failed the technical part of the test I hadn't completely embarrassed myself.

Mike went about correcting what he saw as a major impediment to my survival in the South Bronx. I couldn't fight. I could do all right against other amateurs, but sooner or later I would get hurt by one of the many truly talented fighters in the Bronx. He knew that to be a successful street fighter in the South Bronx one had to have more than heart. He knew I would never learn how to fight unless I conquered the fear that makes you panic when you get hit hard. He knew that many fighters "lost it" under pressure and began to resort to blind punching, leaving themselves open to being taken apart by a trained fighter. Therefore it was necessary for me to fear him during our training sessions. The fear made the training more realistic. I would be expected to defend myself knowing I might get hurt at any moment.

Slowly, over time, I began to learn the science of combat. Mike was a tough teacher, but he was good. I learned how to bob and weave, jab, hook, throw combinations, and to take shots to the head and body. With my increasing skill my status on the block began to change. A lot of the boys Mike's age began to accept my hanging around. My peers knew that I was now someone to be reckoned with, and challenges to me grew few and far between.

I began to hang out and even to travel with the older boys off the block. I became known as their "chaser." Being a chaser meant that I went to the store to buy their cigarettes, beer, or whatever else they wanted. I preferred hanging out with them more than with kids my own age, and soon I was accepted as a member of their group.

Being with Mike, Junior, and the other older boys was a constant challenge. There was always a new lesson just around the corner.

Chapter Eight

●

Test Questions

There was nothing particularly different about this afternoon. As usual, the block was alive with activity—children playing on the sidewalk, some of the guys playing stickball, people just hanging out on the block, talking, drinking, smoking cigarettes. I was playing checkers with Melvin, who was much older than me and lived several blocks away. He and I had become friends in much the same way Mike and I had. He was friends with Mike and Junior and was their age, but he was in the Navy and often away. In many ways he was a reluctant warrior. Bigger than everybody else but gentle, Melvin seemed to reflect the basic conflict that most of the young men struggled with—how to be decent and yet get respect from those who weren't.

As Melvin and I played checkers, a small group gathered to watch and to listen. Melvin was talking trash while we played, a mixture of curses, exaggerations, and good-hearted teasing. Because Melvin was fond of me I was spared his sharpest wit, which could cut you like the K55 knives that some of the older guys carried. I was no slouch when it came to street banter, and used my slight size and young age to my advantage.

Melvin started in, "C'mon, goddamn you, gonna take all day? Ain't gonna make no difference. Shit. Study long, you study wrong. You big long-head motherfucker. Quit leaning your head over the board. It's so big it's blocking the sunlight."

I responded, "Yeah, you talkin' so much shit you missed a double jump. That's all right, my head might be big because it's filled with brains—why's your ass so big? King me."

"I'll king you, but when I finish busting your ass you're gonna wish you were the queen. 'Ohh, jump me. Ohh, jump me.'" Melvin displayed a limp wrist and strutted around imitating some of the more obviously homosexual young men who sometimes visited the block. The others laughed, some doubled over holding their stomachs as Melvin pretended he had a wand and crowned me the Queen of Union Avenue.

It was important that you not let others get the best of you in these trash-talking contests. I was losing bad, so I had to go to dangerous territory. "That's all right, I know why you think I'm the queen. It's because your mother thinks she's a man. She got your head all fucked up. *I'm* a man, *I* got the dick—remember that. I keep trying to tell your mother she ain't no real man. It's your move."

"Playing the dozens" was always a tricky business. If the two involved weren't true friends, a fight was sure to ensue. My being so small and young and talking about Melvin's mother made what I said funnier than it truly was, and less provoking. Melvin responded in kind about my mother, with those listening letting each of us know when one had scored a good solid hit by their laughter or cries of "Ohh, man!" This kind of talk could go on for hours, with others jumping in so the original players became spectators.

Melvin had me so engaged in both playing checkers and trying to respond to his cracks that I barely noticed everyone's eyes suddenly shift and the laughter die down momentarily. Melvin's eyes held mine and he pointed behind me with his chin, lifting it ever so slightly. I turned my head nonchalantly, knowing that whatever was happening called for discreet viewing. I saw a man we all saw from time to time passing through the block. We knew him as "the numbers man" and he sold most of the numbers in our immediate neighborhood. He was limping slightly but moving with a purpose. He was heading down Union Avenue right past our game, toward 168th Street. In his hand he held a small silver pistol. It was the first gun I had ever seen. I found it strange that he would be coming down our block with a gun out in his hand. Being the youngest there, I watched the others closely to see if it was time to run. They looked on with what could only be called mild amusement. No sign of fear, no sense of panic. I decided that I too would play it cool. I acted like they did, as if nothing of particular importance was happening.

I had actually looked back down at the checkerboard and was trying to figure my next move—I was taking the acting too seriously—when I heard the silence. Everyone suddenly stopped talking. I looked up in time to see the numbers runner coming back toward us, gun still in hand, his attention riveted across the street. When I looked across the street I couldn't believe my eyes. A girl that I knew from elementary school, who couldn't have been more than sixteen, was in the middle of the street with a rifle. I was so shocked I couldn't move.

The numbers runner, using us for cover, started up the steps next to the place where we had our checkerboard set out on the back of a car. The girl aimed the rifle. I stared. In a flash I came back to my senses. The rifle looked like it was aimed right for my head. I panicked. I turned and ran up the steps to hide in the hallway. It felt like I was running in slow motion as I waited for the bullet that I knew was on its way to slam into my back.

I didn't hear the gun go off. I was in a sprint, running down the hallway, heading for the back stairs to the alleys in back of the building. No one, and I mean no one, could catch me once I hit the alleys and their fences, which I could scale while running full speed.

It was with the certain knowledge of escape that I almost met my death. I wasn't the only one who knew of the protection offered by the web of alleys. If you were willing to scale walls and squeeze through holes in fences, the alleys could lead you to exits too numerous for one person to cover or predict. I had forgotten about the other antagonist in this drama. As I rounded the corner to the stairs leading down to the alley I almost bumped into the startled numbers runner.

I am alive today because he was a seasoned professional, not a scared kid with a gun. I could see he was as shocked as I was, having someone running up behind him like that. The small-caliber gun came up so fast it was a blur to me. It took me several seconds to even realize that a gun was pointed at my head, and by that time he had shaken his head, said, "Shit!"—as in, "Shit, I almost shot a stupid kid"—and continued down the stairs and out the doorway to the alley.

Certain that the girl with the rifle was only seconds away from coming down the hallway blasting everything in sight, I turned and bolted up the stairs, two at a time, stopping only when I got to the fifth floor. There I kneeled on the steps, trying to hear if someone was coming up the stairs but finding it difficult to hear anything over my labored breathing and the pounding of the blood in my ears. My heart felt as if it was trying to burst from my chest.

I waited. In my mind I was trying to figure how long it would take someone to search the hallway. I could visualize her silently tiptoeing up the stairs, finger on the trigger, tense, scared, ready to shoot anything that moved. I waited. Time seemed to stand still. How long had it been—ten minutes? Twenty? I couldn't tell.

Finally I decided that it was impossible to know how long someone might wait in ambush for another person. I had to go back downstairs. I began to whistle—the careless, tuneless whistling of a little boy. Even a scared girl with a rifle would recognize the sound of a child, and that might make her hesitate in pulling the trigger long enough for her to verify that I was not her target. So down I came, whistling as loud as I could, landing after landing. Finally I came to the first floor, rounded the corner, and . . . nothing. I walked down the hall toward the stoop. My eyes had grown accustomed to the dark hallway and I couldn't see anything but the glaring midafternoon sun when I looked out of the vestibule into the street. Was she still waiting? Would she be aiming into the building from across the street, too far away to hear my whistling?

I walked into the sunlight, blinking and straining to see what awaited me. I saw exactly the same things going on as before I'd left. People were playing stickball up the block, others were standing around talking, drinking beer, laughing. The checkers game was being played on the same car trunk. Melvin was still playing, still talking trash. I wanted to shout to the block, "Listen, I almost died in there! I could be dead lying in the hallway and no one would have even bothered to miss me. Didn't anyone notice I was gone?"

I knew that under all circumstances if you were going to hang with the older boys you had to be cool. So I was cool. I fixed my face, which meant I removed all traces of fear and rage from it, put my foot up on the car's bumper, and began to watch the game. During a break in the action Melvin noticed me and asked where I'd gone. I told him I'd run into the building when I'd seen the rifle pointed at me. His response was "What are you, *stupid*? Don't you know you hit the ground when someone points a gun in your direction?" And he looked at me with the same look my teacher used when I got a low grade on a test. A look that said, "I'm disappointed in you, I thought you were smarter than this." I thought to myself, How in the world was I supposed to know that? It seemed like all the other kids knew it, but where did they learn that lesson at? Once again I wondered if I would live long enough to learn all the lessons necessary to survive in the South Bronx.

Hit the ground—sound advice when someone is pointing a gun in your direction but you are not the primary target. Hit the ground, as all soldiers are taught to do when they come under fire. Not a bad test question for use in our urban schools:

> When someone points a gun in your direction but doesn't want to shoot you in particular, you should
> A. run into the nearest building.
> B. yell and scream while you run away.
> C. stand still.
> D. hit the ground.

Most kids that I know get this question wrong. They usually choose B or C. I learned the right answer from Melvin: hit the ground. Each week I read how another innocent child is shot while amateur gunmen blast away at targets real and imagined. It's a sad state of affairs in this country when starting in kindergarten we need to teach our children their ABCs, but more importantly what to do when they hear shots or see people pointing guns.

* * *

It was only a few years later that Melvin was shot. He was trying to stop another man from beating one of his female relatives. The man pulled a gun. Melvin tried to run. He was shot in the back. He lived the next twenty years in a wheelchair, paralyzed from the waist down. He was never the same. The bullet destroyed more than his ability to walk. Being crippled at such a young age robbed him of his youth, and finally of his will to live. He died in that wheelchair, another casualty of Union Avenue.

Chapter Nine

●

Having Heart

Mike had always told me that if you ever face a gun your actions should be based on how the gunman acts. If he is sure and in control, he is probably a professional; do what he tells you and you might live. If the gun shakes in his hand, if he's loud and nervous, you have a real problem. These are the signs of an amateur and you can never tell what an amateur might do, so be prepared to fight for your life.

There is a reason I worry about our children in the summertime. Most of the times I was in serious danger in the South Bronx were during the summer. Our small apartments were like ovens. It was impossible to stay in them during July and August. None of us had air conditioning. Few had jobs. So onto the streets we poured by the thousands—men, women, boys, girls. It was like a street carnival every day. But the evenings belonged to the young men. This was the most exciting time to be out. It could be a quiet night of talk and bragging, or it could be a night that you would never forget. This particular night started out quiet, but stuff had been brewing all day.

I had heard the gossip. Kevin had been drinking earlier in the afternoon with a woman who lived on Union Avenue. The woman was Butchie's mother, Butchie who wouldn't fight. She had other children that we played with, Chicky and Malcolm. We knew that they were poor even by the standards of Union Avenue. The mother was by all accounts an alcoholic, the children left to fend for themselves the best they could. Supposedly Kevin and the woman had gotten into an argument; he had called the woman a bitch and then left. We thought Kevin was wrong, we knew that the woman was harmless and hopelessly addicted to alcohol, but as was the way on Union Avenue when none of the rules of conduct on the block had been broken, we left Kevin to deal with his own conscience.

Later that night a group of about six of us were sitting on a small stone wall. Everyone was talking and laughing, seemingly content to just enjoy the company of one another. A quart bottle of Rheingold beer was being passed around. If people had plans they had not been announced. Often nights like this one ended with us just going upstairs one by one until the block was left to the warm summer night. I was with the older boys, Mike, Junior, B.J., Kevin, but the group was a fluid one, people coming and going as the night wore on.

We all looked toward the street when a car came screeching to a halt fifteen yards from where we were sitting. A few eyebrows were raised but we continued to talk. Then out came the man. You couldn't help but notice him. He was at least six-foot-three, and huge. None of us could have gotten our arms around his waist. He weighed at least three hundred pounds. He stormed over to us, anger gleaming from his small eyes. "I'm looking for a guy named Kevin. You know where he is?"

Kevin, standing right with us, looked puzzled. We all knew the drill, never admit to anything concerning anybody else's business. The answer was automatic. "Naw, never heard of him."

The huge man began to walk away and that would have been the end of it, except something came over Kevin. I have seen young men do this time and time again (and little did I know that fifteen minutes later I would be doing it myself)—that is, take on a challenge with no hope of winning, simply because a threat to one's "manhood" couldn't go unanswered. Kevin called to the man's back, "What you want with Kevin?"

The man turned and approached us, his wary eyes shifting from the group to Kevin. "He called my aunt a bitch, and I'm gonna kick his ass. Do you know where he is?"

A couple of the guys began to chuckle, the rest of us tried to hide our smiles. We figured Kevin was in a fix now. He was going to have to lie and say he didn't know anything, opening himself up to unmerciful ribbing from the group for weeks. The rules were you had to fight no matter what the odds were, but none of us expected Kevin to fight this monster. Kevin was not small, but this man made him look like a child by comparison. So we were shocked when Kevin responded, "Yeah, I'm Kevin, and you ain't gonna kick *my* ass, motherfucker."

The man wasn't quite expecting this response. He looked at us and then back at Kevin. I was trying to figure out what was going on because I didn't feel the tension in the air that usually preceded a violent conflict. No one was positioning themselves to help Kevin; as a matter of fact, the group seemed mildly amused. Later I realized that while the group had decided not to sanction Kevin for what was considered a breach of etiquette, neither would it protect him from the consequences of his own actions. And besides, he could have just shut up and let the man leave. So Kevin now had a fight on his hands—no big deal.

The other thing I didn't realize at first was that the older boys had sized the man up and determined that although he was big, he was obviously out of shape and slow. A good street fighter should be able to box him and avoid his blows. It would be a challenge but not impossible for a much smaller man to beat this giant.

Kevin and the man went into the street and with much cursing and fanfare the fight began. It was not much of a fight as fights go. The group had been right about the man. He swung wide, arching blows which were easy to duck. Kevin got caught by a couple of roundhouse punches, but the man was hitting with an open fist. The blows staggered Kevin but didn't do any real damage. The fight dragged on, with the man grabbing Kevin's shirt and landing a couple of good shots. Kevin, hurt by the blows and barely able to reach the big man's face to land a blow, fought back even more vigorously.

The older guys were impressed by Kevin's heart. He had learned his lesson from Richard well. He didn't quit. But it was obvious that neither had he mastered the skills necessary to defeat this enemy. It was decided that the man had extracted revenge, Kevin had fought bravely, it was time to stop the fight.

I was sitting with the others, amazed. I had been sure that we were allowing Kevin to face a severe beating, but the group had been right to let the fight go on. Kevin was a little bloody, but he was on his feet fighting. I was happy we were finally going to end it, though, enough was enough. It was Mike who announced, "All right, that's it." And with that all of us got off the wall and walked into the street, Mike and Junior yelling that it was over.

The man saw us coming and announced that the fight was not over, he was going to "fuck this motherfucker up." "No, this fight is over. You won," he was told simply. "Now if you don't stop we're gonna kick your ass. That's it." The man could tell we weren't playing. He didn't like the odds of six against one. Kevin was still trying to fight and the man held him off with one hand as he began to retreat. Before we knew what happened he began to run. He ran to his car, opened the trunk, and came back to us walking quickly. Even before I saw it I knew by the way he walked that he had a gun. My knees got weak and I hoped I would be able to run when everyone else began to flee. I looked at the others and my heart sank.

As the man approached us with the gun, the group began to fan out in a wide circle. I couldn't believe that no one had any intention of running. Kevin made matters worse by saying what most of us would have found comical if the situation had not suddenly become so dangerous: "C'mon, motherfucker. I'm not finished with you yet. Let's fight!"

And so it was that at age fourteen I was thinking of Mike's admonitions about how one should act when a gun was pointing at you and hoping I had learned my lessons well. The group took a step toward the man. The man raised the gun. He pointed it first at Kevin, who began to shout. "Well, shoot me, motherfucker! Shoot me! I'm not afraid to die!" The man looked like he was thinking about it. The group took another step.

The man looked up, frantic. He pointed the gun first at one of us, then at another, turning in a half circle to be sure we all knew he had a gun. "I'll shoot you motherfuckers! Take another step. I'll shoot!" Kevin continued to yell at him to fight like a man. The man seemed to find Kevin's belittling of his manhood too much to take; he put the gun in his pocket and began to fight Kevin again. The guys took another step. It was like I was in a trance. Each time they took a step my feet seemed to move on their own. I couldn't even feel my legs, but when the others took a step I took a step at the same time.

I thought we were acting suicidal. Yet I couldn't run. To run would mean I would lose all respect from the guys, respect I would never get back. So I had to hope. I had to hope that he'd shoot one of the others first and that in our rush to close the distance I wouldn't be the second person to get shot. The way everyone was tensed I knew that if he began to shoot we were all going to rush him from all sides—the classic "you might get one or two of us but we'll get you" theory.

These days the man simply would have blasted away at us, knowing that not to do so would probably cost him his life. These days, in this kind of situation, instead of one person with a gun there would be at least two, meaning that a gunfight would be almost a certainty. But this was 1966, and America's inner cities had not yet turned into the killing fields that they are today. While it was clear that we ruled this block, that we were some of the toughest guys the Bronx had produced, none of us owned guns. Back then a man could pull a gun on a bunch of street toughs with a fair amount of certainty that he had the only gun on the block.

But even in 1966 having a gun didn't mean you could terrorize young men who had faced terrors so often that they wore their lack of fear as a badge of honor. My friends had grown up making decisions at an early age that might have meant life or death for them. When you grow up like this something changes. Some part of your basic humanity you hide down deep lest it be trampled into the dirt again and again and again. You become what we used to call cold. Being "cold" meant you displayed no emotion during times when others would be terrified. These guys, my friends and protectors, had never been given a break. They had no illusions about fitting into a world that had turned its sharpest edges to them every time they tried to struggle up and out of the South Bronx. They weren't mean, but they were tough. They weren't hateful, but they were "cold." They loved one another enough to be willing to die, to sacrifice themselves, but love was a word you would never hear them say. Kevin was not a favorite, but he was one of the group. And it was all this that I saw and understood when I was growing up, and it changed my life.

As Kevin and the man fought, the group took another step forward. The man pulled the gun from his pocket and yelled, "Get back! Get back, I'm gonna shoot!"

Everyone stopped, no one moved backward. Then a funny thing happened to me. I knew that death was close, real close, but I realized that there was nothing to do about it. I had given up the option of running. That freed me to act. I was still petrified, but my mind was no longer racing all over the place. I now knew what I had to do and that brought a certain calmness to me. The facts were that we were going to jump this man, take his gun, and probably give him a beating that would leave him close to death. I wasn't going to do it, *we* were. I understood. We were a team, acting in concert. Two things would trigger our charge, him shooting one of us or the group getting close enough to launch a desperate rush, with luck before he could shoot more than one of us.

I looked out of the corner of my eye and saw the concentration on Mike's face. He was our leader and he was unafraid. He wouldn't take unnecessary risks, but it was clear that he intended to take the man out. I realized that when I had first faced the gun I'd felt like the hunted, but really we were the hunters. I wasn't the only one who felt this. The man began to understand the plan. He knew he had misjudged. The gun hadn't scared us off. He was confused and the circle was tightening, beginning to close off his retreat. We all saw the fear come into his face as he began to back up toward his car, the gun swinging wildly from one of us to the other. We stopped. A trapped man is more likely to shoot. He kept the gun trained on us as he opened the driver's side of the car, ducked in, and roared off. Never to be seen again.

As I watched the car disappear down Union Avenue I thought I was going to faint. Once again I wondered, What kind of world was this where one minute you could be laughing and joking, the next you could be facing death? Walking toward the group that had gathered back on the wall, I was eager to start the conversation about what had just transpired. There was so much to talk about, so much to say.

"Geoff," Mike said, "go get us another quart of beer." He turned to the others. "Listen, let's play Home Street in stickball tomorrow. They say they got some money together and if we can raise twenty-five dollars they'll play." That was it. No talk, no analysis, no nothing. I went to the grocery store to get beer for the guys, my legs still shaking. Just another night on Union Avenue.

Part II

●

A Matter of Time

Chapter Ten

•

America's Secret War

While it can be argued that ours has always been a violent nation, in recent history Americans have been slaughtering one another in record numbers, in what can only be called America's secret war against itself. This war's chief victims are our children; tens of thousands of them have been killed by guns over the past decades. The fact that this war has been allowed to get so out of hand has a lot to do with whose children were thought to make up the majority of those tens of thousands killed. In the late seventies and eighties the victims were thought to be almost exclusively poor and minority. More recently there has been a recognition that children killed by handguns are just as likely to be white and from working-class and middle-class communities. This has prompted a new round of national attention and new calls for action.

Guns have contributed mightily to the escalation of this slaughter. According to Children's Defense Fund estimates, "There are more than 270 million privately owned firearms in our country—the equivalent of nine firearms for every 10 men, women, and children." Greedy handgun manufacturers and lax government regulations have helped precipitate in this country a crisis of unimagined proportions.

I listen with concern as one suggestion after another is proposed as the one cure-all for dealing with violence among the youth of America. One-shot gun buy-backs, tougher sentencing for youth caught with guns, so-called boot camp programs, quick-fix conflict mediation, metal detectors in schools—the ideas go on and on while the complexity of the issue of violence is ignored and the death toll continues to rise.

Part of the problem is that most current policymakers fail to address the problem of the sheer availability of guns. Young people in our inner cities know that there is a war going on; millions have been accidentally or intentionally caught up in the many small battles that make up the war on America's streets. Most young people are interested in surviving the war, but the price they pay is being prepared to kill or be killed almost every day.

As the number of guns available to young people has increased so have the odds that they will be shot in a confrontation. Many young people have figured out that the best way not to be shot is to shoot first. It makes sense, if you live in a war zone, to have a gun for protection, especially if adults, police, and parents seem incapable of protecting you. Most young people I know who carry guns do so for protection. They don't want to be victims, and they feel the only way to have a fair fighting chance is to own a gun. The rules of conduct on when to shoot, or when someone else might shoot you, are unclear. In some places there has to be a physical conflict, in some a nasty verbal conflict or just a wrong look can get you shot, and in some places you could be shot just for being there.

So think about it. Here you have tens of thousands of kids with guns, trying to protect themselves, but there are no clear rules to follow. This is not like the Wild West, when you squared off with your opponent and said, "Draw." Sometimes these days they yell and curse and then shoot you, sometimes they just shoot you.

I knew that the codes of conduct were deteriorating when I heard young teenagers saying they'd "rather be judged by twelve than carried by six." The message on the street is clear: make a preemptive strike, shoot first even if you're not sure that your life is threatened at that moment. Odds are you'll live, and if you're arrested and then convicted at least you'll still be alive. Take it one step at a time: first stay alive, even kill the other person, then worry about the rest.

So many of our young people live under vicious, mean, and violent circumstances. They react as I did when I was young, they don't tell their parents, teachers, or other adults about the constant and real danger they face. They figure out survival skills for themselves, or seek the advice of their peers or older kids.

It's hard for me to forget how violent the world of children can be. I have a permanent reminder, a small little something that ensures I will remember the tough choices too many of our children have to make.

My mother has beautiful fingers, long and thin. I was often told I had inherited my mother's hands. She told me what an asset her long fingers had been when she'd learned how to play the piano. I can see my mother's hands when I look at my fingers—all but one of them. When I look at my right index finger, not straight like the others but with the last joint jutting off at a right angle, it reminds me of the Bronx, of an earlier time when my priorities were clear and simple: don't ever be a victim again.

There is no real pain from the finger, sometimes just a dull throbbing. Most people don't notice it, and I'm used to taking a ribbing from friends about it. My football coach in high school used to say my bent finger was the reason my passes wobbled when I threw them. My teammates on the basketball team called me "Hook" because when I signaled play number one while dribbling the basketball with my left hand, my right index finger didn't point toward the ceiling but toward my teammates.

Adult friends often wonder why I don't simply have surgery to get the finger straightened out. I tell them it doesn't bother me or limit me and I really don't notice the finger after living with it for all these years. But the truth is, the finger keeps the urgency of the work my colleagues and I do with children at the forefront of my mind. The slight deformity is such a small price to have paid for growing up in the South Bronx. So many others paid with their lives. Many who are still alive are addicted to drugs, or are in jail, or are HIV-positive, or are debilitated by mental or physical injuries—

all traceable back to the South Bronx. I feel so lucky to have only a part of one finger as the toll I paid to make it out. But I don't want to forget what life was like. There was a time when getting out of the South Bronx was a distant dream, one you kept far in the back of your mind. Fear and the struggle to survive were ever-present realities. The finger is my reminder of what young people are willing to do for protection.

The year was 1964 and I was in the sixth grade at P.S. 99. I had learned my lessons well both in school and on the streets. I found school, though, to be the lesser challenge. I loved reading, and my mother, who read voraciously too, allowed me to have her novels after she finished them. My strong reading background meant an easy time of it in most of my classes. The streets were a different matter. I had fought enough to have gotten a reputation as one of the smart kids you'd better not mess with. I was becoming more and more serious about sports, and found my slight frame getting stronger and stronger each month. Mike was teaching me to box, and the other boys knew that I could handle myself with kids my own age.

Still, there was the problem of the older boys and the tough blocks where they congregated. At twelve years old I was beginning to travel around the Bronx more and more by myself. When I was with the older boys from Union Avenue I could travel with no fear, but by myself or with peers I was always worried about other older boys robbing us, boys who were quick with their fists and always on the lookout for likely victims.

There were two parks where we liked to go to play basketball or football, and both were several blocks away. To get to them we had to walk past places where boys we couldn't beat lived and preyed on boys like us. The humiliation and shame of being victimized time and time again was almost too much for us to bear. Watching someone saunter down the block with your money—or your new basketball or baseball glove, knowing it would be another year before you could replace it—filled us with a rage for which we had no outlet. It was a violation of body and spirit to be "chumped off" by young thugs. You confronted the worst parts of yourself at these times—your fear, your vulnerability, your cowardice. Back we would march to Union Avenue, our heads hung in shame, our most prized possessions lost. I knew I couldn't live like this. Some kids stayed victims but I knew this wasn't for me. As fate would have it, I literally found my answer.

The K55 knife was the weapon of choice among the older teenagers of the South Bronx. It was about ten inches long when opened, with a five-inch blade. The blade was long enough to do real damage, the knife when closed was thin and easily concealed in the pants pocket. The K55's blade locked into place when it was opened and would remain locked until you pressed a button on the handle that allowed it to fold again. It was not a switchblade that flew open with the press of a button—you had to manipulate this knife with two hands, one to pull out the blade by its edge while the other held the handle. There was a distinctive click when the blade locked in the open position.

I found my first K55 in the gutter. One day I was walking with my head down, deep in thought, and there it was. It had probably been lying there for weeks unnoticed. I remember I was barely able to get it open when I first found it, it was all so rusted and dirty. I knew I could never afford to buy a K55—they cost $4.50, a virtual fortune to me—so I couldn't believe my luck. I realized that with this knife came freedom, mobility. If I could get it to work and learn how to use it I could go anywhere and fear no one.

The knife was my big secret. I spent hours cleaning it and oiling it. Pretty soon I had it in perfect working condition. I began to hone the knife and in no time at all it was razor sharp. The knife was more than a weapon; it became a friend to me, the same kind of friend I later heard soldiers who'd been in Vietnam say their M16s were to them.

At this time in the Bronx we walked in a distinctive way that we called bopping. A young man who "bopped" told the world that he was street tough, prepared to fight if challenged. The "bop" consisted of a slight dip on one leg as you walked, arms swinging, fingers held stiff and pointing slightly to the rear, head held slightly to one side.

Often when you crossed into enemy territory you stopped bopping so you wouldn't provoke an unnecessary confrontation. But with my K55 in my pocket I would bop right through groups of boys whose challenging looks questioned my right to travel through their block. The knife was my passport. As I approached a group, my hand would slide into my right pocket to position my knife so that it could be immediately opened, then I would set my eyes straight ahead and wait for a challenge. My movements were not lost on the boys watching me. Most right-handed street fighters kept their knives in their front right-hand pants pockets. When you saw a stranger slide his right hand into his pocket as he approached, this was telltale evidence that he was armed. It was better to leave those armed with knives alone. So although there'd be menacing glares, there was seldom a challenge.

I didn't really know how to use a knife, however. I began to watch the older boys who occasionally took out their own knives and demonstrated different ways to open them to prepare to defend oneself. The primary consideration in learning to use a knife was your ability to get it out of your pocket, opened, and positioned for use in the shortest amount of time possible. Because most of us knew how to defend ourselves with our fists, if you needed a knife in a fight it meant that you were outnumbered or being attacked with a weapon yourself. In either case, seconds often meant the difference between life and death.

I experimented with various means of opening my knife. I decided that the most efficient way was to bring the knife out of my pocket with my right hand straddling either side of the handle so the fingers of my left hand could grasp the half-inch of blade protruding from the handle and pull the knife three-quarters open, then with a flick of the right wrist snap it open all the way. The art of opening this particular knife lay in the fact that it had a spring which pulled the blade back into its handle, but only if the knife was less than half open. Once you reached the halfway mark the blade wouldn't snap back, and when fully opened it would lock into place. The trick of using this particular type of knife was to get your left hand free of it as soon as possible.

I spent hours trying to perfect the removal of the knife from my pocket and opening it as quickly as possible. I started off safe and careful, pulling the blade well past the halfway point to ensure that it wouldn't snap back on my fingers before I let go with my left hand to snap the knife fully open with my right. Over the months I became less and less conservative as I shaved tenths of a second off my time. Finally, after about three months of practice, I became so good with my knife that I could open it to that exact point a hair's breadth past the place where the spring would snap it shut again. To those watching when I demonstrated my expertise my hands moved in a blur. They would hear the distinctive click signaling that

72

my weapon was opened and ready for use even as their eyes tried to catch up with the movements involved; the knife seemed to appear in my hand as if by magic. My performance in delicately balancing speed with precision left no room for error, but few twelve-year-olds are capable of error-free performance for long.

That summer afternoon my practice session had been going well; I thought I'd found a new position that would keep my knife open. I tested it several times. Even though it was only a tenth of an inch different than my usual position, I wanted that extra tenth. The first two times I tried my new method I kept my fingers along the side of the knife's handle so that they would be out of harm's way. After two successful tries I attempted to open the knife the usual way. . . . I knew I was in trouble right away; for a microsecond as I realized the spring was snapping the blade shut I thought I could get my fingers out of the way.

The knife did what it was designed to do, cut through skin and flesh until it reached bone. I opened it carefully. The blood made the blade slippery and I feared cutting myself a second time if it should slip through my fingers and snap back again. My right index finger was badly cut. I knew that I had done major damage because the finger was no longer straight, the first joint was at a ninety-degree angle from the rest of the finger.

I knew that I needed to go to the hospital. But if I went I would have to tell my mother about the knife. She would certainly make me get rid of it, and there would go my protection and my newfound freedom. The alternative was to try to doctor the finger myself. I decided I would rather take the risk of infection than give up my weapon.

I cleaned the bleeding finger with running water. I used our homemade bandaging system to try to stop the bleeding. Whenever my brothers or I accidently cut ourselves while cutting vegetables or playing outside, we wrapped the finger in toilet paper, wet it, and squeezed until the pressure stopped the bleeding. The toilet paper absorbed the blood, and when it dried it would stay in place, protecting the cut. (We usually couldn't afford Band-Aids, so this was how we kept dirt out of a wound.) The problem with this cut was that I couldn't stop the bleeding.

After about an hour of my sitting on the edge of the bathtub, the toilet bowl was filled with discarded toilet-paper bandages. The blood flow hadn't stopped, but it had slowed, so I could at least take the bandage off and examine the finger. I figured I had cut a tendon that held the finger straight. My solution was simple, find two popsicle sticks and use them as a splint to keep the finger straight. The more complicated problem was how to keep all this from my mother. Coming home from work and seeing her child with a finger in a homemade splint made from popsicle sticks would certainly raise some questions.

I decided to tell my mother that my finger had gotten jammed from trying to catch a basketball pass and it hurt me to move it, so I'd immobilized it. A fairly plausible story, since I played basketball almost every day. I just had to make sure that I kept a clean bandage on the finger, so the bleeding wouldn't give me away.

My mother, like all mothers around this country today, had no reason to suspect that her child was armed. I never talked about violence in the house, never shared with her my concerns about my personal safety or about being robbed by other kids. As far as she knew I was having a normal adolescence, filled with sports, girls, and school. She believed the basketball story. I changed the bandages on the finger three times a day, and by the second day the bleeding had stopped. The splint was working and the finger was healing straight.

And that would have been the end of the story if I hadn't decided to play basketball with my friends two weeks later. I was having a great time and was really into the game. There was only one problem—that damned splint kept getting in the way. It was on my right hand, my shooting hand; it had already caused me to miss two layups, and with a tied game my team was depending on me. I took off the splint. My finger when I tested it was a little stiff but seemed fine. I took my eye off the pass, looking for the most direct path to the basket, and felt the ball bounce off my index finger. I knew immediately that I had reopened the wound. Sure enough, when I looked at the finger it was crooked again and the cut had reopened, but it wasn't bleeding nearly as badly as before. I tried to resplint the finger that night, but the next morning it was still crooked. My choice now was to live with a crooked finger or tell my mother about it and go to the hospital. The decision was easy. Better to live with a crooked finger and a knife, in the South Bronx, than a straight finger and no knife. I kept my mouth shut.

It took a lot of energy to hide the crooked finger from my mother, which I did for five years afterwards. I had to be very conscious of how I held my hands and which hand I pointed with. But one of the challenges many of us faced was how to incorporate daily survival techniques into our lives so that they became habits. Hiding the finger was simply another such challenge.

There are children all over this country who are hiding weapons in their closets, in sneaker boxes under their beds, under their sweaters in their dresser drawers. They are certain that they need their guns or knives for their own safety, sure that their very lives depend on having those weapons. We will never convince them to give up their weapons with fancy television jingles or with marches alone. What these children need is a sense of safety, a certainty of surviving as they go to school or to the store.

Whenever I think that I've come upon some quick and easy solution to dealing with violence among young people, I look down at my finger and remind myself that I never really considered giving up my knife. We must come up with solutions that take into account that our children are armed for war and that they will not put down their weapons until we can declare a cease-fire and bring an end to that war.

Chapter Eleven

•

The Drug Trade

That this country has finally realized that violence is a national crisis of unparalleled dimensions is important to me. But it is painful to watch the results, so far, of this realization: billions of dollars poured into prison construction, more police, sexy but ineffective programs like boot camps, and lots of talk about our "war on crime." The problem with these poorly thought-out large-scale initiatives is that they sometimes have unexpected consequences that exacerbate problems instead of helping to solve them. Case in point, one of our last large-scale social "wars," the war on drugs.

While each large city in America had its own version of the war on drugs in the seventies, I think that what happened in New York is particularly illustrative of our American tendency toward quick-fix solutions to very complicated problems.

New York had a very popular governor who served four terms, from 1958 through 1974, Nelson A. Rockefeller. In response to the hysteria about drugs that permeated society and was highlighted by the media in the early seventies, Governor Rockefeller pushed through legislation that came to be referred to as the Rockefeller drug laws.

On the surface these laws made a lot of sense. Drugs, in particular heroin but increasingly cocaine as well, were a national scourge. There seemed to be a revolving door in our criminal justice system when it came to drug dealers. Cops lamented that they were barely done with the paperwork before the dealers were back on the street. The state seemed powerless to stem the tidal wave of drugs coming into New York. So Governor Rockefeller proposed laws that would create minimum mandatory sentences (fifteen years to life) for possession of relatively small amounts of narcotics. This law was coupled with a "second felony offender" law that meant that if you had one felony and were convicted of another within a ten-year period you would receive an even longer mandatory prison term.

The idea was simple enough: get tough on drug dealers and drive them out of business, or at least out of New York State. But the Rockefeller drug laws had several unanticipated results. One of these, not widely recognized even by social scientists and criminologists until recently, was the creation of a whole new employment market for young kids. As the Rockefeller drug laws began to have an impact in poor communities, drug dealers began to realize that being caught with drugs on them could mean doing the rest of their adult lives in prison. Selling drugs in poor communities has always meant being out on the street so that your customers can easily find you. Being on the street with drugs during the Rockefeller years made dealers vulnerable to police sweeps, operations in which drug agents would suddenly drive onto the block and arrest them before they could ditch the drugs or hide.

The answer many dealers came up with was as simple as it was evil. They began to use children. And many children were eager and willing to be used in such a fashion. Poverty always provides these willing children, whose lives are haunted by tattered clothes, empty refrigerators, broken dreams, nerves of steel, and toughened hearts. In many communities drug dealers are looked up to by children who lack other role models. Young boys are especially susceptible, as they associate the power and wealth of the drug dealer with making it as a man. So the dealers found no lack of willing boys to help them avoid the long jail sentences that awaited them if they were caught selling drugs.

A further reason boys became such a boon for adult drug dealers was that if the boys were caught with drugs they would go into the juvenile court system, which generally was more lenient on youngsters caught with drugs than was the adult system. And the juvenile could sometimes get caught over and over again without major ramifications. Even if the juvenile got sent away to one of the locked facilities, if he was a "stand-up guy" and didn't "snitch," when he came home he received more respect and more status on the block than he'd had when he went away. This newfound respect might actually help him consolidate his business, as his new reputation led other young dealers to respect him.

When I first became aware of the large-scale movement of children into the drug industry, they were mostly acting as lookouts and steerers. The lookout and steerer job was basically to stand on the corner and keep an eye open for the police and the dreaded undercover narcotics officers. These children were an early alarm system, giving the older dealer time to escape or hide the drugs. They also "steered" customers to the dealer, often having the drug user wait while they took the money to the dealer and brought back the drugs.

And so in the mid-seventies a slow but steady stream of children thirteen, fourteen, fifteen years old began to enter the drug business. Heroin was still America's narcotic of choice, and while the number of heroin users in this country was at an all-time high, a dealer needed only a few children to help look out and steer users. We probably would have had a small but serious problem, somewhat exacerbated by the imposition of the Rockefeller drug laws, but for a new drug that was on the rise and would blow up our inner cities like an atomic bomb.

Cocaine was a popular drug in the late seventies and early eighties. America was still not convinced that it was addictive, and the use of cocaine still carried a certain glamour among the "hip." In poor communities, cocaine was certainly present, but its high price (it was usually sold in fifty-dollar packages) meant that it was at most an occasional treat for some inner-city residents. It seemed that "sniffing" cocaine, while addictive, takes some time to create a real habit, so generally residents of the inner city were at most occasional users of cocaine; marijuana, angel dust, and heroin were more popular in this population. The dealers had a highly select and fairly regular customer base for cocaine, but usually one or two people selling it were enough to handle that customer base.

Crack cocaine changed everything, seemingly overnight. As crack came on the scene in the very early eighties no one seemed to be aware of the devastating influence it would have on our communities, especially on poor communities. For many of us who work with children, however, its impact soon became obvious. We began to notice more and more of our young boys being killed.

As more and more children moved into drug sales, one of the first things they began to recognize was that they were in a dangerous business. Because guns and the drug trade go hand in hand, it didn't take long before children involved in the trade began to want guns and to buy them with their illegal profits. Guns were not everyday tools during the early years of children selling drugs. By and large children were off limits to rival drug dealers who wished to murder or intimidate another dealer. But in a business where status plays a major role in being able to do your job, a gun was increased status. And these children, too, often fell prey to older boys who would stick them up for their money and jewelry. A gun was an added layer of protection.

Still, guns didn't become commonplace among the young until crack use became epidemic in the eighties. Several separate accidents of history created the love affair that today's young people have with guns. The first was the unintended consequence of the Rockefeller drug laws—bringing children into the drug trade. The second was that crack cocaine is a drug so addictive that in a matter of a few years there were millions of Americans addicted to it. The third factor was the relatively low cost of crack. A crack high could cost as little as two dollars, making it affordable to millions of poor people who could not afford the powdered version of cocaine. This increased demand and created a huge employment market for young people to work the streets to feed the ever-growing hordes of addicts who came for crack morning, noon, and night.

The sums of money that young people received from selling crack in some cases were enormous. It was not long before young people who had once been content to be lookouts or steerers wanted a more significant role. They wanted to run the business, and began to recruit their friends and peers to form their own "crews" to sell drugs. These young people made thousands of dollars many times over, but they could not spend it on what the older dealers did—cars, homes, businesses. They were simply too young to be able to purchase such things, so they spent their money the only way they could, on designer clothes, expensive sneakers, and gold jewelry. And, as could only be expected, other kids began to rob them of their clothes, sneakers, and jewelry. The answer for almost all of the young dealers was to buy a handgun for protection.

And, slowly at first and then with more and more frequency, young people in and out of the drug trade began to arm themselves. Where once handguns had been relatively scarce commodities, in a very short time they became ordinary. The young dealers not only set the fashion trend with their expensive clothes and gaudy jewelry, but they also began to set the violence trend. The handgun had replaced the fist or knife as the weapon of choice. The codes of conduct on the streets across the nation were about to undergo a major and lethal shift.

Chapter Twelve

•

"Rep"

For decades it seemed that we in America saw nothing wrong with poor kids fighting for what they believed was right. When I was growing up, *The Bowery Boys* was a television show we in the South Bronx all watched and enjoyed (in spite of the fact that the only black Bowery Boy was the most afraid and the most marginal of the characters). Each episode always had the classic fight scene, when the boys who were thought of as a street gang rose to fight for a higher good. We related to the Bowery Boys because they were poor like us and, like us, they were willing to fight when it was necessary. *The Bowery Boys* was just one of the shows we watched in which sooner or later violence was the way to achieve what the characters wanted.

A steady stream of violence as the answer for the powerless was spoon-fed us via television and the movies. *The Dirty Dozen* showed us outcasts in prison who through their toughness and criminal past outwit and outfight the Nazis and become heroes (of course Jim Brown, the only black, dies; this was before any black could be a hero on screen). In *Death Wish*, a man who has had enough with waiting for justice kills those who have wronged him and his family. Then there was Bruce Lee, who could out-punch or out-kick ten men at one time and was always willing to fight when the powerless needed justice.

And those of us in America's ghettos—the poor, the powerless, the trapped—we worshiped at the altar of violence. If we had nothing else we could still act as men. Not the kind of man who runs and hides when trouble inevitably comes knocking, but the kind who rushes toward trouble ready, willing, and able. We despised those who accepted the humiliation of being pushed around, insulted, robbed. No, we believed in being real men, men like Leo Gorcey, who was small but always willing to fight bigger men. Men like we saw in the movies—Bruce Lee, Superfly, and Shaft, ready to fight and if need be to die for what they believed in.

To us these violent movie stars had the ultimate in "rep," as we used to say. And we had other role models closer to home. Those who were really tough, ruthless, and fearless made reputations for themselves that were known throughout the Bronx. Many of these men became the drug sellers and major criminals in our neighborhood. The criminal underworld was then the domain of men, some in their twenties, some older; young boys played no significant role in drug dealing or other serious crimes when I was growing up in the mid-sixties.

These older men, although often ruthless, did not kill indiscriminately, which is what saved my life in my encounter with the numbers runner and his gun. They used violence to ensure that others didn't try to take advantage of them—rob them or move in on their territories. Their reputations kept all but the foolish, desperate, or most vicious from crossing them. This meant that most of us had nothing to fear from them. We knew they were gangsters, but they were businessmen gangsters. They preferred to do their business out of sight, and their primary interest was making money.

Today we know that this trend has reversed. Young men, many of them young teenagers, control most of the street dealing in our urban ghettos. Often these are not the really tough kids who drifted into crime after years of gaining a "rep" on the streets. For many of today's child gangsters, how tough you are is measured by how lethal a gun you carry. They may never have won a fight, or even fought one; if you are willing to carry a gun and use it, you qualify to sell drugs. Having no established reputation, most of these dealers are subject to hostile takeovers by other, more ambitious dealers. Today's drug seller is often a child who was one day hanging on corners, never having had a job, and the next day got recruited.

I began to notice these inexperienced, unsophisticated child drug dealers in the early 1980s, when I left Boston and returned to New York to work at the Rheedlen Centers for Children and Families.

In 1983 I ran one of the programs at Rheedlen that was designed to work with children whose parents had abused or neglected them. We also worked with children "at risk" and with neighborhood children who just needed a place to be after school. At that time Rheedlen ran programs in several schools in Harlem and in upper Manhattan. I was responsible for about two hundred children, and I watched many of them grow up. I unfortunately knew too many who are no longer alive. Many of these kids are dead because they should never have gone into the drug business. They were silly kids, kids like most teenagers, not very serious, not dependable, who made poor, impulsive decisions, definitely not seasoned toughs who knew the score.

The first time I heard that Charles was selling drugs in his project in Harlem I didn't believe it. This kid was downright immature and much too silly. He was not what I would call a tough kid, although he knew the streets; I felt no self-respecting drug dealer would entrust to him their "product." Which only shows I wasn't yet aware of how the drug industry had changed since I had left New York City in 1974. The mid-level supplier (who had always been an adult when I was growing up) was now likely to be a kid himself and just as likely not to have the kind of experience needed to run a drug business, to be able to tell who he should hire, who could be trusted, what were the relevant characteristics of a good employee. The dealers now took just about any kid they knew wasn't a cop and who said he wanted to work. Boys like Charles, who any adult could tell was not serious enough to hold even the most basic job, ended up working on corners selling drugs.

When it was brought to my attention that he owed money on the street,

I knew that, as improbable as it sounded, Charles at fourteen really was selling drugs. I needed to act, and quickly. I met with Charles and got the facts. He owed a little more than a hundred dollars. He said it was no big deal. I told him how serious it was, that he would be made an example of if he didn't turn over the money and "cop a plea," and promise never to do it again. I implored him to get out of the drug business. He listened politely to me, and nodded his head as if he was agreeing with me, but I could tell it wasn't sinking in. I told him how he had to live now that he was a wanted man, how he should avoid his building and usual haunts until he had paid back the money. He told me he could get the money, "no problem." He just seemed not to take the whole thing seriously.

Several weeks later they caught Charles in a hallway and shot him many times, mostly in his legs. He was one of the lucky ones; he was to be an example, but a living one, of what could happen if you were found stealing money. Charles was the last kid I knew who would live after being caught in the open by the new breed of child gangsters.

Over and over again I would be told, "Geoff, you'll never believe who's selling drugs." And it was true; I couldn't believe it. Like Charles, the kids named would be the most unlikely of drug dealers, silly kids in a deadly business. The funeral parlors have become rich as a result of their poor decisions.

Take Hector, for example. I knew him for years as a member of our Center 54 afterschool program. Always a wise guy but never really a problem, Hector was well liked by all. He was a joker, not serious about much of anything. I first suspected he was selling drugs when he came in one night after I hadn't seen him for a couple of years. I was happy that he had dropped by. He was limping and walking with a cane. I asked what had happened; he said, nothing, he was in an accident.

I later learned the truth, that the accident he'd had was a car pulling up next to his on the street and his being shot at point-blank range by the people in it. The other occupant in his car had been killed. He'd been taken half alive to the hospital, where he was informed that people were trying to get to him even there to kill him. I'd had no idea that he was a major supplier of drugs in the neighborhood. Other young people I talked with told me he was quite an investor. It was said that he owned several buildings and a couple of supermarkets in Manhattan; at nineteen he was already rich and had the world on a string. I was amazed to find all this out. There he was, knowing people had tried to kill him and were still looking for him, and he had walked into the center openly, no bodyguards, no secrecy. I couldn't see how he would live long taking chances like that. They killed Hector on the street three weeks later.

Chapter Thirteen

●

Self-Defense

While violence has been a factor in our slums and ghettos for decades, never has it been so deadly. Today children face the almost impossible task of making life or death decisions all alone, in a matter of minutes, sometimes seconds. Even those of us who have been lucky enough to survive enough violent encounters to have gained an amount of expertise in dealing with violence find the current codes of conduct to be so harsh, capricious, and variable that it makes it almost impossible to help young people cope with the everyday violence they face on the streets and in schools. Today many children grow up in a waking nightmare of sudden death around every corner.

I have spent decades working with poor, minority children from some of New York's most dangerous communities. I spend some of my time teaching them a form of martial arts called tae kwon do. Originating in Korea, tae kwon do is a means of self-defense that emphasizes kicking techniques. Years ago I realized that for many children living under the constant stress of violence, martial arts offers not only a respite from fear and a sense of personal power, but a way of teaching discipline. The study of tae kwon do also provides a forum for discussing violence and strategies for avoiding violent confrontations.

The martial arts were once a means of providing for one's personal safety but, as I tell my students, not anymore. The gun has replaced all other means of aggression and defense. The proliferation of the handgun in our inner cities has meant that physical ability, courage, and determination are no longer the critical components in self-defense. Still, there is a growing demand from children to take my martial arts classes. They come for any number of reasons—some for exercise, some because they have nothing else to do, some for self-defense, some because they need something to belong to. The ones who stay do so because they accept the strict discipline, rigorous training, and high moral standards of the school.

Students who have been with me for years are marked boys and girls in their communities. Other young people in their neighborhoods are often aware that they are martial artists. People learn about their training because one of the mandates of the school is that the students must give back to the community. This is often done by putting on demonstrations that have an antiviolence message as their main theme. My tae kwon do students have to walk a fine line in their neighborhoods. Drug dealers and their armed henchmen are used to being looked up to on the block because they are feared. My students are also looked up to, but for different reasons.

Several times a year my senior students and I spend time talking about the pressures they face living in communities where guns in the hands of young dealers, people they don't respect, place their lives in danger. Because they are world-class athletes (many of them have won national championships at martial arts tournaments), and because they do well in school and live a clean life, they pose a certain threat to many of the young gangsters that live on their block. They are seen as the alternative role models to the dealers, so they feel they can't let the drug dealers make them take a low profile on the block. They feel that if children and others who look up to them see them intimidated, ridiculed, or pushed around by the gangsters, it makes it look like there are no forces of good that can withstand the twin evils of drugs and guns. My students have managed to keep respect in their neighborhood, but it's a fine line they walk, and I worry about them every day.

* * *

Even knowing that almost all poor children growing up on the streets of New York City are at risk, I was still surprised when one day the intercom in my office at Rheedlen announced that Robert, the most senior student in my tae kwon do school, had come to see me—it was an emergency. Robert had been my student for over eight years; he was like a son to me. I stopped what I was doing and had him sent into the office.

Like most young people who live with life or death issues on a regular basis, his attitude belied the seriousness of the crisis that he was facing. He approached the issue cautiously.

"Geoff, I need to talk to you about something." I nodded my head for him to continue. "There's this guy who lives down the block. Well, he really doesn't live down the block but he hangs on the corner down there. You know what I mean?"

Well, I thought I knew what he meant. There was a drug dealer who didn't live on the block but sold his drugs on that particular corner. Even in a crisis, young people are cautious not to be branded as snitches.

"Well, this guy is about my age and he had a fight with my younger brother. And he beat him up. He's older and bigger than my brother. My brother might not have been all the way in the right, but still . . . you know? I mean, I had to go see what happened."

Robert knew that in our school we have strict rules against fighting; the only exception is self-defense. And our definition of self-defense does not include going down to confront one of the local drug dealers for beating up your brother. Robert was trying to give me as many of the extenuating circumstances as possible to soften what he knew would be a blistering cross-examination. I just told him to continue, knowing he wasn't here to report on a fistfight.

"Well, I went down there—right?—and I asked him what he beat up my brother for. He told me my brother wanted 'beef' and so he beat him down. I told him no matter what my brother wanted he was older than him and he better not touch him again."

Robert waited. He knew this was the point when I'd interrupt and give him my standard lecture on provoking a violent confrontation instead of defusing one. We'd often discussed the impact of language, how the implied threat of "you better not" was like waving a cape in front of a bull. But this was not a time for lectures. Something had happened. "Go on, Robert," I said in as even a tone as I could manage. I could feel my heart rate quickening—something had gone wrong.

"Well, he told me if my brother came back he would beat him down again and if I didn't like it he would beat me down, too. So I told him, 'If you think you can beat me down, well, come on. I'm standing right here. Do it.' So he threw up his hands and I beat him down."

Robert paused and I began to think. Two kids fighting in the night on a street corner. One kid was a drug dealer, one three months away from testing for his black belt. The phrase "and I beat him down" didn't give me enough information. I asked, "What happened in the fight, Robert? You mean he just fought you straight up? Didn't he know you were a martial artist?"

"Well, at first he tried to fight me with his hands but I was beating him real easy. Then he pulled a knife. So I took the knife away from him and swept him off his feet and I was beating him down when they jumped in and broke it up."

Even for a black belt, defending yourself against a knife is no easy feat. I have always instructed my students that even while I show the most advanced of them self-defense against an opponent with a knife, the odds are always on the side of the armed person. Running away from an opponent with a knife is perfectly acceptable. Robert knew how I would feel about his reckless behavior, but he was still sitting there with more to say.

"OK, what is it? What happened?" I asked.

Robert said in a voice that was almost inaudible, "And yesterday when I was walking up the block this car came up on me real fast, and I heard it and I turned around and they tried to shoot me out the window." He settled back in his chair, having relieved himself of his heavy burden. I know he'd waited over twelve hours trying to decide whether or not to come to me. He'd said "shoot me out the window" so softly that I wondered at first whether I'd heard right. Nothing in his demeanor suggested that he had just escaped death. He wanted to know what to do. Plain and simple, someone had tried to kill him and he wanted to know what to do. He acted as if he hated to interrupt my busy schedule, he knew I was a busy man, but he had a small problem and he needed some advice.

I suggested what any responsible adult would probably recommend. "Robert, you should call the police."

His response was simple and straightforward. "Geoff, this guy is a drug dealer. He's right out on the block. You know how that goes."

Yes, I know how that goes. Snitch on a drug dealer and face almost certain death. Still, the other options were almost as bad. I went through them anyway. "Can you leave the block?" "Can you stay inside until the heat is off?" "Can you have someone else intervene on your behalf?" None of these options was feasible. Robert felt he had two choices—wait to be killed, or kill the other kid first.

I began to question him more closely. "How do you know it was the kid you fought with who was in the car?"

"I saw him."

"How is it you were able to see him? Didn't you hit the ground when you heard the shots?"

"No. I heard the tires screeching behind me. I turned around and saw he was in the passenger side. He pointed a gun out the window and I dropped down behind a car. He shot three times and the car raced down the block."

Now here comes the tough part. I know if I get this wrong, Robert could be dead tomorrow. Young people all over this country have to deal with these types of problems every day. No school offers "Survival on the Streets 101." You can't get an advanced degree in staying alive. No special tutors available, no help after school.

I asked my next question dreading the answer. "Robert, did you look at him? Did you look him in the eye when he pointed the gun?"

"When I heard the car I looked back and saw him. I wasn't afraid and I looked him in the eye. Then when I saw the gun I ducked."

"Robert. Now, take your time and be certain, OK? When he pointed the gun out the window, was he trying to shoot you or was he trying to scare you?"

Robert thought a moment. "Well, I don't think he was trying to shoot me. He pointed the gun in my direction, but he was pointing it too high."

I know how different people who watch the same event even under relatively low-stress conditions often have totally conflicting accounts about what happened. Under a high-stress situation it's easy to miss a key piece of evidence. Having known Robert for so many years and having instructed him on how to respond when under stress as part of his martial arts training, I felt more confident of his recall than I would have of most people's.

My reasoning was fairly simple. By all rights Robert should have been dead. He had no knowledge that the shooter was behind him. Robert was walking and the shooter in the car needed only to pull alongside and blast away. Unfortunately, young men are killed this way every day in our cities. So either the shooter was totally inept or he just wanted to scare Robert and at the same time regain his reputation on the streets. An hour later, Robert and I had decided that the odds were 70 percent that the shooter wanted to scare him, 30 percent that he was trying to kill him but missed. I again told Robert to call the police. He listened politely, said nothing. I knew he had no plans to do so.

Before Robert left we went over the drill for what you should do when someone might be trying to kill you. The drill was a collection of dos and don'ts learned over the years by the mistakes others had made, often costing them their lives: Don't leave your apartment at the same time every day. Don't walk the same way to school. Always survey your block, looking for strangers and occupied parked cars, before leaving your stoop. Always check behind you. And never, never hang out in the same place day after day. I've gone over this drill too many times with too many kids.

After Robert had gone I sat in my office and wondered how many children were in similar situations that day. Who did they have to come to for advice? Would they talk? How many would be dead before the week was out? Would Robert? I had gone over all the strategies with him, talked about every option we could think of, and I knew I had done almost everything I could to keep him alive. With the door still shut I closed my eyes and prayed to God to keep Robert safe. Then I had done all I could do. A year later Robert continued to be fine, but at least six of his peers in that one neighborhood were killed in that same amount of time. One of these was Luis.

* * *

94

I did something I wouldn't usually do in deciding to go to Luis's wake. There are so many funerals for young men who die violently in the neighborhood that I won't go to them unless there is some personal reason to do so. With Luis, since he had worked for me, I decided that I would stop by the wake to try to console his parents. I asked one of my staff members for the address, but ended up going to the wrong place.

When I realized my mistake I decided to go back to 108th Street and Amsterdam Avenue, where there was a small shrine in Luis's honor. These memorials are one of the new things that have sprung up as more young people are killed on the streets. Other young people on the block put up a small shrine where people can come by and pay their last respects. A picture, candles, some mementos—each one is different from the others. I knew there would be someone at Luis's shrine to give me the right address for the wake. Upon arriving, I looked to see if anyone I knew was there (it was close to Rheedlen and my martial arts school). I didn't, but I asked directions from a young man who was standing by the shrine.

"Excuse me, I'm trying to find out where the wake is. Do you know the address?"

The young man turned to me with suspicion. "Who are you?"

I replied, "I knew Luis, and I had the wrong address—" Before I could finish he asked again, taking a step toward me, "Who are you? What you want here?" There was now a clear edge of menace in his voice and I began to pay closer attention to the young man before I answered. I knew something was wrong.

"I knew Luis. He used to work for me and—" Again I was interrupted. "Man, I don't know nothing so don't ask me any questions." The hostility was open now, and suddenly it hit me. I realized I was in serious trouble. You see, I had forgotten a story I had heard a week before Luis was shot and killed.

Three friends from the neighborhood, all teenagers, had decided to sell drugs together. There was some dispute, and before anyone knew what had happened one of the boys had pulled out a gun and shot the other two. One boy was killed on the spot, the other faked death and thereby escaped the certain second bullet to the head he would have received if he had moved. The gunshot wound he sustained was fairly clean and no vital organs had been hit, and the boy had the misfortune to make it out of the hospital in time to attend his friend's funeral. On the way home from the funeral, the boy who had just gotten out of the hospital was gunned down and killed. His assassins had known he would be at the funeral and had lain in wait for him. A dastardly act even for the routinely violent neighborhood these boys came from. This new strategy called for an amendment to the accepted code. Until this point, funerals had been considered sacrosanct. Now the codes allowed for killing even during this once-sacred ceremony.

Having forgotten the story, here I was asking questions about the burial plans for Luis of a person who didn't know me. For all this young man knew, I could be setting up the killing of other people associated with Luis. Once I realized why he was so hostile I became very aware of his every move. If he thought I was an assassin he could very well pull a gun and try to kill me right then and there. I had to make a decision about what to do next, and my eyes strained in the darkness, trying to discern a gun on him. Do I walk away? Or do I try to make him understand that I really knew Luis and I'm no threat?

Just then a young man I had known for over ten years rounded the corner. When I called his nickname—"Choco, over here"—he smiled briefly and came to me and shook hands. The other boy relaxed when he saw that I knew Choco. My heart was pounding and I was glad that the tension of the moment was broken, but Choco seemed even more tense than I was. He told me where the wake was and then warned me, "Geoff, you shouldn't be here standing on this corner. There's a war going on here on this block. Just a couple days ago they came and shot this kid who wasn't doing anything. He didn't sell drugs or nothing. He was just standing on the block. Nowadays if you just stand on this corner you could get killed."

Edward had grown up on the block. His nickname, Chocolate (pronounced the Spanish way), we shortened to Choco, and he was well-liked by everybody. He had had to do what so many young men struggling to make it have to do, remain friends with people he had grown up with who now carried guns and sold drugs, while not getting caught up in the violence that followed them like an ill wind. Even as he spoke to me, his eyes kept shifting up and down the block. I knew Choco wasn't a person who was scared by the streets. I realized we must be standing in the middle of a full-blown war zone.

The car as it approached was moving much too slowly. I knew for sure that something was wrong when I saw the fear in Choco's eyes. He was facing the street and I was facing him, with my back to the approaching car. The young man who had questioned me so intently was also staring at the car. I turned, and my heart felt like it had stopped. The car was still coming slowly, close to our side of the street. The windows were darkened, so we couldn't see inside. The driver's-side window began to go down. We all stooped down, ready to drop behind the parked cars that stood as our only protection.

When I think about it now, it was like a street corner ballet—all of us bending our knees at the same time and the same amount, judging the time it would take us to get our heads below the windows of the parked cars before the guns could come out and find their target. Is it friend or is it foe?

It was friend. A smiling face was driving the car. After calling out a few words of greeting, Choco turned to me and said simply, "Get off this block, Geoff. Don't hang around here." And with that he turned his back and walked quickly away. I turned and went the other way, thanking God that this wasn't my time but not liking my odds. After all, this was a block I had walked up and down for twelve years. I didn't mind thinking of giving my life for a cause, but to be killed just for walking down the street?

I know that people, innocent people, get killed every day in this country just for being in the wrong place at the wrong time. I know this is just the harsh reality of life in the inner city. But I don't want to die just because our country doesn't have the will to act decisively about gun control and violence.

Chapter Fourteen

•

Confrontations

Young people are fascinated by guns. For many today, and especially for boys in our inner cities, the handgun is an integral part of their growing-up experience. It is as important for many of them to know the difference between a Tech 9 and an Uzi as it was for my peers to know the difference between a Chevrolet and a Buick.

And once a young person gets his or her hands on a gun there is a very strong temptation to shoot it. Once you've handled a gun you recognize it as simply a tool. And not many of us get a new tool and put it away unused. Human nature seems to dictate we use them right away, even if we tire of our electric drill, espresso machine, or stationary bicycle soon after purchasing it. So the temptation is almost irresistible for children to shoot off guns in their possession. They want to see what it feels like. What it sounds like. How much damage does it do? How quickly can you fire it? Where can you hide it? How quickly can you draw, aim, and shoot? Every time I read a newspaper story about a child accidently shooting another child with a gun I think about my testing the limits with my knife. My mistake cost me a cut finger—if my knife had been a gun there might have been a dead friend as a result of my foolhardiness.

Even more dangerous than the fact that there are tens of thousands of adolescents shooting and playing with guns is the psychological impact that having a gun has on these kids. There were always some natural checks on violence among young people before handguns were so common. There were many times that I wished I could have fought back when I was growing up but I didn't because I knew I couldn't beat the other boy, or I was afraid of his bigger brother, or he had friends who would come after me. Even when a fight went ahead, the outcome wasn't guaranteed; you might lose, or win but get a black eye or a tooth knocked out. As we got older and more sensible we recognized that there was a system of checks and balances on violence; we learned to weigh acting violently with the consequences. Sometimes, no matter how hard it was to accept, we just had to take the indignity of being ridiculed or cursed at and go on with life.

Kids with guns often see no limits on their power. They have never run up against the natural checks that we faced growing up, when for many of us a broken nose or a cracked tooth tempered our reactions to the daily push and shove of street life. Too often today kids with guns experience the limits of their power only when they are dying. Having a gun means that you can adopt a new set of standards of what you will or will not take from others. Where once if someone bigger than you called you a name you might have mumbled under your breath and kept walking, if you have a gun you will probably stop and confront the person then and there. And you don't have to worry about being outnumbered, because the loud noise that a gun makes almost always causes people to run away from the sound in panic. Possessing a gun feels like the ultimate form of protection. On the streets of a big American city, having this kind of personal protection may even seem to some to make sense. But it doesn't. I know from personal experience.

In 1971, well before the explosion of handguns on the streets of New York City, I bought a handgun. I bought the gun legally in Maine, where I was in college. The clerk only wanted to see some proof of residency, and my

Bowdoin College I.D. card was sufficient. For a hundred and twenty-five dollars I was the proud owner of a .25-caliber automatic with a seven-shot clip. The gun was exactly what I needed. It was so small I could slip it into my coat pocket or pants pocket.

I needed the gun because we had moved from Union Avenue to 183rd Street in the Bronx, but I still traveled back to Union Avenue during holidays when I was home from school. The trip involved walking through some increasingly dangerous territory. New York City was going through one of its gang phases and several new ones had sprung up in the Bronx. One of the gangs liked to hang out right down the block from where we now lived, on 183rd Street and Park Avenue. When I first went away to school I paid no mind to the large group of kids that I used to pass on my way to the store or the bus stop back in the Bronx. The kids were young, fourteen or fifteen years old. At nineteen I was hardly worried about a bunch of street kids who thought they were tough. But over the course of the next year the kids got bolder and more vicious. On several occasions I watched with alarm as swarms of teenagers pummeled adults who had crossed them in one way or another. Everyone knew they were a force to be reckoned with, and many a man and woman crossed the street or walked around the block to keep from having to walk past them.

And I crossed the street also. And there were times that I went out of my way to go to another store rather than walk past the rowdy group of boys who seemed to own the block. On more than one occasion I rounded a corner only to come face to face with the gang. I could feel their eyes on me as I looked straight ahead, hoping none of them would pick a fight. That September in 1971, when I got back to the serenity of Bowdoin College, I was more tense than usual. I realized that those kids had me scared. After having survived growing up in the Bronx, here I was scared to go home and walk down my own block. The solution was simple, and as I held the small gun in my hand I knew I had found the answer to my fears.

After a few target-practice sessions I lost interest in the gun. It was simply a tool to me. In Brunswick, Maine, it was a useless one. There was no reason ever to think you would need a gun for protection in Brunswick. So I unloaded the gun and packed it away and forgot about it. The only time I remembered it was when I thought about going home, and it was the first thing I packed when I headed back to the Bronx for winter break.

Things had only gotten worse on my block during my four months away. The kids were more organized and more threatening. There seemed to be more of them than before. But that didn't bother me; I was a changed man. I had a gun. I had a gun, a seven-shot clip, and an attitude.

When I look back on the power the gun had over my personality and my judgment I am amazed. It didn't happen all at once; the change was subtle. At first I continued to avoid the gang of teenagers. I crossed the street or turned down another block when I saw them. But slowly, as I carried the gun with me day after day, my attitude began to change. I began to think, "Why should I have to walk an extra block? Why should I feel that I have to cross the street or look down when I pass those kids?" By the end of two weeks I had convinced myself that all of the habits I had cultivated to avoid conflict with the gang were unnecessarily conciliatory.

My behavior when I went outside began to change. I stopped going out of my way, or crossing the street, or avoiding eye contact when I passed the gang. In fact, I began to do the opposite. I would *choose* to go to the grocery store on the side of the street where the gang was gathered. I would walk through them head up, eyes challenging, hand in my coat pocket, finger on the trigger. I was prepared to shoot to kill to defend myself. My rationale was that I was minding my own business, not bothering anyone, but I wasn't going to take any stuff from anyone. If they decided to jump me, well, they would get what they deserved.

I was lucky that winter break. Time quickly came for me to go back to college and no member of the gang had felt the need to challenge the strange young man with fire in his eyes and his hand always in his coat pocket. Away from the madness of the South Bronx, the gun again became just another useless article from home that I wouldn't need until it was time to go back. The serenity of Maine helped me think through the transformation. The same gun, the same person, but a totally different relationship between the two depending on the environment. In Maine the gun was extraneous to my daily existence, in the Bronx the gun was a crucial part of my psyche.

I knew if I continued to carry the gun in the Bronx it would simply be a matter of time before I was forced to use it. My behavior would become more and more reckless each day. Carrying the gun had been like becoming a superhero. Suddenly I'd had power, real power. It had been intoxicating. I thought long and hard that year about carrying the gun. In the end my Christian upbringing proved to be stronger than my fear of the gang or my need for a sense of control over my environment. In the end I realized that I didn't want to kill anyone. I knew that if I continued to carry the gun I would sooner or later pull the trigger. I unloaded the gun, wrapped it in newspaper, took it to the town dump, and threw it away.

In 1971 I was one of the few teenagers walking around with a gun on the streets of New York City. Today young men with guns are the rule in some areas of New York, not the exception. These are young men who are carrying guns for protection and status, not necessarily to shoot someone. And yet, these are young men who because they are armed feel less inclined to avoid confrontations that could escalate into bloodshed. The power of the gun is no less intoxicating to them than it was to me. The evidence of their need to carry a weapon for self-defense is made clear to them every day as they talk about who was shot, who was robbed, who was killed. They are not going to swap their guns just for sneakers, or gift certificates, or small amounts of cash. And unfortunately for us all, many of them have not been raised in the church or with any moral teaching, so the fact that they might end up taking a life is not a persuasive argument for throwing away their guns.

In an old African American spiritual one verse runs,

I'm gonna lay down my sword and shield
Down by the riverside . . .
Ain't gonna study war no more.

I used to sit in church as a child and wonder what war was being studied. Today there are many young people around this country who have known nothing but war and have studied hard. It's time to do something while we still *have* time.

Part III

●

The Best Way We Know How

Chapter Fifteen

•

Free-Fire Zones

I returned to New York in 1983 armed with the experience of years of working with some of the toughest adolescents in Boston, my degrees from Bowdoin and Harvard, and my recently earned black belt in tae kwon do. I felt that because of my professional development in New England, and because of how I grew up, I was ready to come back to "prime time"—New York City—and make a difference.

I was hired by the Rheedlen Centers for Children and Families that summer. Rheedlen was then headed by Richard L. Murphy, who had founded the organization in 1970 as a truancy prevention program for children between the ages of five and twelve. Over the years, Rheedlen's mission expanded with the expanding needs of poor children and their families, first to working with families, then to include an entire neighborhood. In 1997, we expanded yet again, this time to develop a network of programs for a much larger twenty-four-block area. The Harlem Children's Zone, as our organization was renamed, today encompasses nearly one hundred blocks, serving thousands upon thousands of children and adults. Richard

Murphy, who would go on to be commissioner of the New York City Department of Youth Services under Mayor David N. Dinkins, had dedicated his life to saving poor children in Harlem and in other pockets of poverty on the west side of Manhattan. I recognized the same passion and commitment to poor children in him that I felt myself, and I was ready to go to work.

> Dear MR KeNNedy
> I'm very sorry what happened on friday october 30, 1992.
> It was all A big misunderstanding
> Me and my 3 Brothers and A frend was on our way to the Motivation Room when we ran into Mr Baxter And we had a brife conversation durning the conversation Al Happens to mention to be careful and grasb his croch where the toy gun was and Mr. Baxter thought is was real and went and told Mr. Alfonso that we came to kill Mr. Mills But we didn't. . . .
> So please let me back in the Motivation Rm.
> I asure you it will never happen again. I need the motivation Rm alot.
> Thank you
> Sincerly yours
> Raheed

I smiled when I received the note. The misspellings and poor grammar were signs that Raheed had written the letter to me himself. I remembered the call. I remember all the gun calls. So much is at stake when the issue is children and guns.

One mistake in judgment and someone's life could be lost. Yes, I remember all of the guns calls, even though they come in much too frequently. This one was tough. Alfonso Cayetano, the director of Rheedlen's Motivation Room program, had called to tell me about a threat three boys had made toward one of our social workers. The boys hadn't liked a decision made to suspend another boy from the after-school program. The threat was clear: one of the boys had pulled up the front of his shirt to display the handle of a gun stuck in his waistband and had warned the social worker to "be careful."

Once again we at Rheedlen were faced with the most difficult of situations: what should we do about children with guns? These boys had just become teenagers and were basically good kids. I had to make a decision. I decided to play hardball. I had Alfonso call the police, call their mothers, and suspend them all from the Motivation Room. When you are working in dangerous communities, the children, especially the young boys, must learn that you cannot be intimidated by a threat of physical harm. In these situations, all the other children in the program are looking to see if you will stand up to the most dangerous and aggressive children.

While I will never carelessly place the children or staff around me in additional jeopardy, neither will I allow children or adolescents to run us out of a community or make us change our norms and values because of the threat of violence. The HCZ exists because there must be programs in communities that have felt abandoned, left to be ruled by those with the biggest guns and the least regard for human life. Children need to look to adults for a sense of protection and security. If all they see is young men with guns setting the normative standards in their communities they will naturally accept those standards as their own.

One of the answers to the plague of violence in America is the approach that the HCZ and other community-based organizations have taken. This problem cannot be solved from afar. There is no way that government, or social scientists, or philanthropy can solve this problem with a media campaign or other safe solutions operating from a distance. There *is* no safe way to deal with the violence that our children face. The only way we are going to make a difference is by placing well-trained and caring adults in the middle of what can only be called a free-fire zone in our poorest communities. Adults standing side by side with children in the war zones of America is the only way to turn this thing around.

Our organization has been recruiting social workers and youth workers who are willing to go where the need is greatest and so, by definition, where the danger is greatest. We know we're on the front lines when we get the calls and have to make the tough decisions. What calls? The ones you hate because lives are at stake. And if you stay in this business long enough, you know that sooner or later you will get the call that someone has been shot.

When I first talked about coming to Rheedlen, I remember feeling that the job seemed perfect for me. But I raised one concern to Richard Murphy during the interview: I had to run a martial arts school. I explained that I had experimented with teaching inner-city kids martial arts in Boston as part of a violence-reduction strategy and that I was convinced that the discipline and values taught in martial arts could help young boys and girls resist the constant peer pressure to fight and act violently. I knew it seemed counterintuitive that teaching young people how to punch, kick, and defend themselves would *reduce* violence, but I had seen firsthand the peace that many young people had experienced, some for the first time in their lives, after time spent learning martial arts.

I thought that my insistence on teaching martial arts might prove to be a stumbling block to my taking the job at Rheedlen. But I was dedicated to reaching as many young people as I could, and I knew there was a certain segment of the population that I could only reach in this way. I remember how serious and solemn I was when I told Murphy all this. I mistook his smile for an indication that he thought it was a minor matter. He was smiling, in fact, because Rheedlen ran an after-school program at a junior high school right down the block from our main offices, and he thought it would be great to open a martial arts school right there, for the young people who lived in the neighborhood.

The director of the after-school program was Joseph Stewart, a young man who had dedicated his life to serving the troubled youth in a very poor census tract of Manhattan known as Manhattan Valley. The junior high school where he ran his program was smack in the middle of Manhattan Valley and was named Booker T. Washington Junior High School 54. We all called it by its number, J.H.S. 54. Joe embraced my desire to offer a martial arts class there, and in September of 1983 I opened up the Chang Moo Kwan Tae Kwon Do Club in the school's basement.

My tae kwon do school stayed open at the junior high all through the Rheedlen years, and it continued and even grew with the founding of the Harlem Children's Zone. The classes stayed free, and I worried and fussed over my students like a mother hen. Even today, my fears for these boys and girls are grounded in a sad reality, one that first sank in when I returned to New York and saw how drastically things were changing for the worse. After a very short time I realized that death circles over the ghettos of this country like a huge eagle, seemingly coming from nowhere, plucking our children from our midst suddenly and without notice.

When I look back on my first years at Rheedlen, I realize how clearly I saw the signs of what was coming. I began to try to get others interested in what I knew was an impending explosion of violence. But the violence hadn't yet crept out of our poor communities and into the more affluent neighborhoods around the country, and there seemed to be little outside interest in what those of us located in these communities began to dread—the end results of handguns in the hands of teenagers.

Daily I worried about getting a telephone call late at night that would carry the awful news that one of my students had been shot. The first of these calls, when it came, wasn't for one of the children in my martial arts class but for one of our staff.

I had not been home long that evening when Richard Murphy called. "Geoff, I have bad news. They just shot Joe. The ambulance has taken him to the emergency room. We don't know how bad it is. I'll call you back when I have more information."

Murphy hung up the phone, and I knew we had several problems. Our most pressing concern was for Joe. I was relieved to find out fairly quickly that he would be all right. The bullet had struck him in the backside and wouldn't cause any permanent damage; he would be in the hospital for a while and then at home convalescing. But Joe was loved by the adolescents who came to Center 54. At six-foot-five and over two hundred pounds, Joe seemed an imposing figure only until you got to know him. He loved his kids and they loved him back. His shooting would not go unpunished. Many of the center's members considered Joe family, and if someone shoots someone in your family you must avenge that dishonor.

I knew that Joe's shooting would have a powerful effect on the neighborhood. There would be anger, outrage, and fear. The first job we had to do was counter the rumors that began to circulate around the neighborhood more quickly than we could keep track of them. The most serious rumor was that Joe had been killed. We knew that there was already a group of young men looking for the shooter, and that they had stated he would be killed on sight.

We began to collect the facts. There'd been a neighborhood party at Center 54 that night. Joe knew that for our children there were few social outlets, and he had been in the habit of throwing dances for them so they could socialize safely. The dances could easily draw two to three hundred kids; we had tight security and they were always fun events for the community. This night an argument had ensued between two teenagers and one had been asked to leave the dance. He came back with a gun, looking for the boy he'd had the argument with. While standing outside, Joe heard the teenagers yelling, "He's got a gun! He's got a gun!" and began to herd the boys and girls back inside the school's doors. There was one boy who was a little slow to go inside, and as Joe lunged to push this last boy in, the assailant opened fire. Joe had taken the bullet aimed at that boy.

Joe's heroism made the neighborhood adolescents even more intent on seeking revenge. They knew he had risked his life to try to save one of theirs. It was decided that the shooter would have to pay, and the word was out on the street that he was a dead man. We figured that Ramon, a neighborhood boy who was one of the most respected adolescents in the community, was the crucial link in trying to stop the cycle of violence. Ramon's brother had been the target of the shooter.

Ramon and I later became good friends, but I hardly knew him when I was given the assignment of trying to talk him out of the revenge killing that we heard he was vowing. He was typical of so many of the young men who grow up hard in New York City—the oldest boy, the "man of the house," responsible for the protection of his family. He was what we called "no joke," as in, "You know Ramon, he's no joke," which meant he was an honest, law-abiding kid who lived by the codes of conduct on the street: leave me alone and I'll leave you alone. But he was a fierce fighter, and if anyone tried to take advantage of him or his family he was prepared to fight to the death—no joke.

What made the situation even more dangerous was that Ramon was well loved by the gangsters in the neighborhood. They loved Ramon because he was an exceptional athlete, and because he was fair and nonjudgmental.

He knew that many of the boys he grew up with sold drugs for a living. He chose not to. He carried himself with a pride and a swagger that made little kids on the block look up to him, not the dealers. The dealers understood this, and they also knew that Ramon was not afraid of even the most dangerous of them. They carried guns, but Ramon would not be intimidated by them and they had to treat him with respect. He was a local boy gone good, and even the drug dealers saw him as a role model, if not for themselves then for their little brothers. This meant that there would be others who would see it as their duty to kill the person who had tried to shoot Ramon's brother. They knew that Ramon was not a criminal, had no criminal record. They would kill the boy as a favor, so that Ramon would not risk ruining his life. I knew the hunt was on and that time was running out for the kid who had shot Joe.

Upon meeting him, I realized that Ramon was someone you respected immediately. Quiet-spoken and earnest, he explained that times had changed. "These days these punks get a gun and they think they can just shoot anybody. The only thing they understand is 'If you shoot me, you better kill me, because I'm gonna kill you.' Then they stop and think about shooting you. That's why no one shoots Ralphie." (Ralphie was a notorious drug dealer who controlled the crack in the neighborhood. Considered invincible, he was known to have killed several people. He himself would be killed seven years later.) "They know if they mess with Ralphie they're dead. Even if they kill him, they're dead. These punks don't have the heart to face death. They get a gun and they just think they can shoot you and get away with it. Once we get finished with this punk no one will ever try to shoot Joe or anyone else from the center. They'll understand the law of the streets protects them. We have our own rules. Forget about him. He broke the rules, he pays the price."

After three days of pleading, I finally got Ramon to agree not to carry out an act of revenge. But he explained to me, "Well, you don't have to worry about me. *They're* gonna get him. I don't have to lift a finger. You just can't go around shooting people these days and expect no one is going to shoot back. Especially if you're a punk like him. If they let him get away with that, everyone will think they can just go get a gun and start blasting." Little did Ramon know that in five years the world he described would be the new reality on the streets: everyone with guns, blasting away. But in 1984 a different code of conduct still surrounded the use of a gun.

For several days there were young men looking everywhere for the boy who'd shot Joe. I am convinced that the boy's arrest saved his life. But trying to stop others from killing him wasn't our only concern. At Center 54, student morale was crushed. Their favorite adult had been shot. It looked like violence could come anywhere and take anyone. There was an air of crisis in the center, and all the kids were wondering who would come and restore calm and a sense of law and order.

Richard Murphy and I recognized that the two days right after Joe's shooting would be critical. The adolescents would be sure to test whoever came in to manage the center in Joe's absence. I knew from past experience that violence of this magnitude had a real impact on how kids would behave. They'd be acting tough to mask their fear and concern for their own safety. They would resent any adult who tried to replace Joe, because he had been there for years and had developed a loyal following among the teenagers.

I knew Richard Murphy and I had the same idea. I volunteered, to keep him from having to ask me. My task was clear to me. The staff, children, and volunteers were in shock. One of our own had been shot while on the job. Everyone began to ask themselves, Could I be next? Is it safe to work here or go to the center? I had to try to restore a sense of confidence in the staff as well as in the children. Even though I had been teaching my martial arts classes for some time, classes were in the evening, and most of the youth at the center did not know who I was. The afternoon after Joe was shot I walked over at 3:00 P.M. There was already a large gathering of students at the entrance, waiting for staff to let them in.

The boy was about fifteen years old and standing at the top of the stairs to the entrance of the center. All the other kids were watching him. The knife he was drawing arcs in the air with was a 007. I was familiar with that model. It was one of the biggest folding knives made and was popular with the many young people who felt bigger was better. The knife had a seven-inch blade that folded into an eight-inch handle. When extended, the knife was over a foot long.

The boy and I locked eyes as I walked up the stairs toward him. He made no attempt to hide the knife, and, in fact, took pleasure in placing me in the position of either confronting him about his weapon or ignoring it and going inside to safety. All of the others there on the stairway wondered what I would do. After Joe's shooting did anyone doubt that young people were dangerous and could cause harm, even to those adults who were there to protect them?

I knew this confrontation would be the talk of the center for days. I didn't relish what I would have to do, but I knew too much was at stake not to. I came straight up to the boy, and before he could think, I was within stabbing range. If he assumed that waving an open knife would intimidate me, I wanted him to know in no uncertain terms that it did not. I wasn't being completely foolhardy—my training in the martial arts had taught me self-defense techniques against a knife attack. But I had no desire to get into a struggle where certainly someone would end up severely injured. Luckily, the boy had unknowingly allowed me to take away some of his advantage with the long weapon, which was distance. I was now close enough to grab his knife hand and take control of the weapon at the slightest sign of aggression.

As I expected, the boy was completely flustered by my approach and my attitude. I was acting as if his knife was a cigarette or a dirty magazine. I scolded him: "What's the matter with you, sitting there with that? What kind of a center do you think we're running here? You think I'm gonna let you come in here with that? There are no weapons allowed in here, and if you don't turn that over right now, you're out. I mean out for life."

I turned to the crowd that couldn't quite understand why I seemed not only unafraid but not even nonplussed by the huge knife. I seemed to ignore the boy, not even to be looking at him, as I turned to the group. I always kept my attention focused on that knife, however, even if my eyes seemed to concentrate on other things. I was prepared to defend myself at the slightest sign of an attack. To the group of teenagers gathered I said, "If I catch any of you bringing a weapon in here, or if I see any fighting at all, I'm gonna throw you out of the center. Joe has been shot because someone *stupid* used a gun." When I said the word "stupid" I looked at the boy with the knife. He had stopped waving it and now didn't know what to do.

I continued, "Joe's going to be all right. He'll be back in a couple of weeks. Until then I'm in charge here. We will have a safe center."

To the boy with the knife, who still didn't know quite what to do, I turned and whispered, "Put that knife away now, and if you ever plan to come back in here bring it with you to my office." With that I turned and walked into the school and stood guard as each child signed in. The boy with the knife did come to my office and pleaded to keep the knife. I was adamant that he give it to me or get kicked out of the center. Reluctantly, he gave up the knife. Center 54 remained calm, its members sensing that even though violence had entered one of the few oases they had, order had been restored.

Joe Stewart came back to work in a few weeks and showed no hesitation at being on the front lines again. Joe and people like him are the real heroes in our communities. After a short period of time he even started having dances again. He knew that the young people had no other place where they could go to socialize.

Our concerns about security grew each year after Joe was shot. There seemed to be a war raging around us. Every time we turned around we heard of another young person getting shot, and they were dying of their wounds more frequently. In 1991 we held our last community dance. By that time we were using handheld metal detectors and searching the persons and handbags of all entrants.

The fight that ended our community dances happened after that last dance was over. Members of our security team went to break up a fight outside. A young boy who was arguing with another boy pulled a handgun. He pointed it at the two members of the security team who were on their way to intercede and they stopped in their tracks. He pointed at the boy he had been fighting, who covered his head with his hands and tried to dodge what he knew was coming. The boy with the gun pointed it at the other boy's head and followed his movements. The one with the gun seemed indecisive. The other boys around him started yelling, "Pop him! Pop him!" He didn't know what to do. The other boy continued to flinch and try to dodge the bullet he was expecting at any second, his hands still shielding his face, as if he didn't want to see death charging at him from the barrel of the gun. The boy didn't shoot. He put the gun back in his waistband, and the other boy, seeing that he would be spared, ran out of sight.

It happened that two of my martial arts students were the security team that came to break up the fight. They explained to me that they knew it was all they could do to save themselves when they saw the boy point the gun toward them. They told me how the other boys, fourteen and fifteen years old, had shouted, "Pop him!" and how the crowd had seemed disappointed when he didn't pull the trigger. I couldn't fathom how casually the crowd wanted to see someone shot and probably killed. I thanked God that the boy had had the good sense not to shoot. But I also knew that the next time he pulled a gun on someone, there would be tremendous pressure from his peers that this time he use it.

Chapter Sixteen

●

The Sit Down

Shawn Dove was one of the codirectors of a community center located in Central Harlem. Shawn was on the phone and we had a problem. There are times when you are psychologically prepared for the problems that working at a place like our organization can bring into your life. At other times you are not. This evening I wasn't prepared for anything more challenging than a quiet night with my family. Shawn's call interrupted what had been a very tranquil evening.

Shawn explained that some of the young men from the block had stormed past our security post and were in the gym, threatening staff and refusing to leave. These men were in their early twenties, and we had been negotiating with them for several weeks about the times they could use the gym to play basketball. Somehow the dates had gotten confused and they thought this was their night. When they were told that they couldn't come in, they "bum rushed" the security post, went upstairs to the gym, and told the staff they would shut the program down if they weren't allowed to play.

As Shawn and I talked, it became clear that the situation had already gotten out of hand. There'd been cursing and pushing, and one of our staff had been threatened. It was up to me to decide what to do. This particular program served over a thousand children and adults every week, and I was determined that no group was going to shut it down. I knew it was risky and could backfire on me, but I told Shawn to call the police and have the men escorted from the building. Shawn did just that.

As fate would have it, after making their point—that they could force their way upstairs if they wanted and there was nothing we could do to stop them—the men decided to leave on their own. They were walking down the stairs just as the police were coming into the building. When they realized that the police had been called, they became enraged. In many African American communities the police are looked upon as the enemy, and calling the police on someone is treated by some as tantamount to being a traitor.

Shawn's second call to me that night was to inform me that the men had now threatened to kill members of the staff—most particularly Shawn and the other codirector, Joe Stewart—because we had called the police. Shawn made it clear to me that there was real reason to be concerned, because some of these guys were probably involved in illicit activities, and they all owned guns or had access to them.

Guns and sudden death are a real hazard in the business I am in. So far, my staff and I have been fairly lucky, but I know that the odds are against us. Sooner or later, if things stay the same, one of us will be badly hurt, or even killed. I wanted to try to manage this crisis from my apartment in Harlem, but I could hear in Shawn's voice that this situation was extremely dangerous.

I tried to get from Shawn the kinds of facts that experience has shown me are necessary to properly evaluate a violent situation: How many potential assailants were there? Where were they presently? How angry were they? Who were their likely targets? The answers I got back confirmed my worst fears. There were about ten guys. They had left the building, but they habitually hung on the corners right down the block. They were "pissed off," and there was cause to suspect one or two might carry out their threats against staff in general and Joe and Shawn in particular. The situation was very fluid, and no one could predict what might happen.

Being the director of an agency like mine calls for unusual skills. I found myself thinking more like a military strategist than a human services executive. First, I told Shawn to have all the children and parents in the building leave immediately. They were not to be frightened; we would simply tell them we had to close the building early. Shawn was instructed to have all of the female staff leave with the others. My experience told me if there was to be bloodshed, it would be the males that would end up being the targets; the codes of conduct still protected women and girls under most circumstances. I told Shawn to call the police and request a squad car be stationed outside the building. That ought to afford some protection for the male staff on their way home.

I thought in passing about how tenuous our ability to do our work could become. The last thing I'd told Shawn was that our work was too important for anyone to stop it and that, no matter what, we'd be there tomorrow, running the program. I thought about what I meant by "no matter what." I called Shawn back. "I'm on my way over. Tell everyone to stay inside until I get there."

The drive to Seventh Avenue and 144th Street seemed too short. I was trying to think back to the time when I really knew the streets. Back when I could size up a group hanging on a corner in an instant and decide friend or foe. But I had lived many years where my life didn't depend on the subtle cues that those who lived on the streets could read like an encyclopedia.

I went around the block once and saw scores of young men hanging on the corner of Seventh and 144th. I couldn't help thinking that one of these men could end up taking the life of one of my staff, or my own. My spirits surged when I saw the police patrol van, but as I turned the corner to circle back to the school I saw the van pull off and head down Seventh Avenue. I have never felt so alone. When I came down 144th Street and pulled up next to our school I prayed to God to protect us. I thought, "I'm getting too old to be running toward the guns." I'd thought it was a stupid idea when I was a kid in the Bronx, and it didn't feel any smarter now.

When I arrived at the school, our young security force came immediately to surround me. I couldn't help but notice the irony; I had come to try and protect their young lives, and without thought these kids now risked themselves to shield me from the most likely source of gunfire, Seventh Avenue.

I knew how to walk when you're trying to let potential foes know that you're unafraid. I hadn't forgotten that. I strolled toward the small knot of staff that had waited for my arrival as if I hadn't a care in the world. It was important for them, too, to think I was unafraid and confident.

Both Joe Stewart and Shawn Dove were outside the front door when I arrived. They informed me that the situation had stabilized. One of our staff, a young man named Jackie who had been raised on the block and knew most of the men who had threatened us, had gone to meet with them. Jackie, who is an extraordinary young man we call the Pied Piper of 144th Street because of the way the teenagers respect and follow him, was just walking back to us to report on his meeting. He said, "I went down to the corner and told the guys that they could shoot me if they wanted, but I had to tell them that they were wrong to threaten to shoot anybody who worked here." Jackie had negotiated a "sit down" between the men and me, as they still felt that Joe and Shawn had been unfair to them.

What Jackie did still haunts me, and reminds me that often the actions of an individual can mean the difference between life and death. I was happy to agree to the sit down and commended Jackie for taking such a risk. I supervised the closing down of the building for the night and made sure that everyone left 144th Street safely. Try as I might, I could not get our young security team to leave before I did. They loaded me into my car and watched me drive off the block. A braver group of young men and women I have not met. I felt we had all won a small victory that night.

But the angry young men aren't the real enemy. There is another, maybe even more powerful than the ones—poverty, drugs, hopelessness—we confront and combat on a daily basis. There is another force aiding the slaughter of thousands of our young people, a force that until a short while ago I knew nothing about.

Chapter Seventeen

●

Targeting Children

I have had some sleepless nights and I've been filled with anger and rage since I learned certain truths about guns in America. The revelation came at a dinner meeting at the house of children's advocate Marian Wright Edelman.

It was the subject of violence that had brought Marian and me together in the first place. In 1990 she had decided that violence was an issue that the Children's Defense Fund, the national advocacy organization that she heads, had to get more involved in. She started a series of forums around the country so that she and her staff could meet and talk with people who were dealing with this issue on a daily basis. It was at one of these forums that I presented my views on violence to Marian, and that was the beginning of our friendship.

Marian convinced me that I had to join the national movement she was spearheading, the Black Community Crusade for Children. At first I resisted. I was already overcommitted. I felt she didn't understand well enough that *my* children in New York City were *dying*. I didn't resist long. Marian *did* understand. She understood about my children and about children all over this country. More importantly, she felt the pain of their suffering. It was personal to her.

It is this pain that drives me as well. I still feel it. The pain of being scared. The suffering of poor children as they try to cope with a world that crashes upon them like a tidal wave, drowning so many, and so many washed out to sea to flounder and pray for rescue. A rescue that almost never comes. Marian still feels their pain. The pain of a nation of poor children. Too much for one person to bear. Ending this pain is her mission. Her cause. Her reason to be. I felt that I had found a mentor, a soulmate.

I had learned that you never know what might happen at dinner at Marian's house. She and her husband, Peter Edelman, were constantly using every resource they could muster to make life better for children. At times there just weren't enough hours in a day, so dinner meetings had become part of the strategy. It was at one such gathering, in the fall of 1993, that Senator Dodd from Connecticut, Senator Simon from Illinois, a couple of key government officials, and a couple of advocates (I was one) met during a time of active debate on anticrime legislation. Marian knew that the Senate was working to put more than $20 billion into the new legislation, now known as the Crime Bill, to build more jails, hire more police, and create more boot camps. There was little discussion of prevention in the bill.

The senators were interested in what we thought could really make a difference in reducing crime, especially violent crime, committed by youth. We debated and shared ideas over dinner and coffee, staying late into the night. From that meeting grew the Ounce of Prevention Fund, a senatorial crime-prevention initiative written into the bill. Ninety million dollars was targeted for preventive services and strategies for children in the fund. I shake my head in amazement when I think of how important that dinner at Marian's was for the country and for our children. And I recall that dinner now because it's useful for all of us to remember just how transformative it can be to bring compassionate people into the same room to talk about what really matters. That kind of conversation can change the world.

Soon afterward I was invited to attend another dinner meeting, this one called for those of us who were part of a national antiviolence network. Again, the meeting was at Marian's house, where we gathered to hear from the director of federal policy for the Violence Policy Center, located in Washington, D.C. The Violence Policy Center had as its central focus the need to regulate the firearms industry. What we were told that night shocked and appalled me, literally raised goose bumps on my arms.

The presentation itself was fairly straightforward. The center had been studying the firearms industry, and one of its findings recognized that the industry had gone into a slump in 1983 and decided to change its marketing strategy. The following is a quote from *Cease Fire: A Comprehensive Strategy to Reduce Firearms Violence,* written by Josh Sugarmann and Kristen Rand:

> A separate article in the same issue [of *American Handgunner*] entitled "Handgun Market Is Down Not Out," continued the lament: "There is no question that the handgun market is experiencing a depression unlike anything encountered before. Many manufacturers have reduced production staffs and many wholesalers are either in deep financial trouble or have already left the scene."
>
> Reasons offered for the plummeting sales included increased sales of used guns, decreased exports and an actual shrinking of the market. Eventually, it became clear that the slump stemmed from saturation of the primary market of white males.
>
> The 1983 handgun slump taught the industry that it could not take sales for granted and forced its members to rethink how they marketed their product. To improve sales they took two tacks.
>
> The firearms industry decided to:
> • Expand the market beyond white males with the new target markets being women and youth. A niche marketing plan was undertaken similar to that employed by cigarette and alcohol manufacturers.
> • Redesign and expand its product line.

I listened in horror as it was explained to us how a campaign had been created by gun manufacturers to increase the use of guns by children. Part of the new strategy was to give assault weapons and handguns names that young people find enticing, like Viper, and to appeal to their belief that bigger is better. The Saturday Night Special was back with a vengeance, now in the form of a semi-automatic that held more bullets and was lethal on the streets. There was a new demand for nine-millimeter handguns and assault weapons, some capable of holding fifty to a hundred rounds. And even these were being sold over the counter like hairdryers. Smaller weapons were produced cheaply, the .25 semi-automatic being one example, making them affordable to poor youth throughout America.

Here I was dealing with children dying every day and trying to solve the problem on the streets, and other Americans were sitting in offices designing new and more effective ways to entice children to use handguns. I looked at Marian Wright Edelman and the look of disgust on her face told it all. How could this be going on? How could people design a product especially for children when they knew those same children were being slaughtered all over this country with that product?

I became curious about how much our young people at Rheedlen knew about handguns. I gathered a group of adolescent boys and girls together and asked them some questions. They knew. They knew more than I had imagined. They knew the names—Tech 9, Uzi, Glock 17, and on and on. They knew where to get them; they knew what they sounded like; they knew how much ammunition each held. They discussed these guns with the same intimate knowledge that the boys I grew up with discussed cars and car engines. They also bought gun magazines. They were fascinated by guns, and, in the same way we looked forward to the new-model cars each year, they looked forward to the new models of handguns, with their new gadgets and high-tech sophistication.

Guns were easy to buy on the black market even in New York, which had one of the toughest gun laws in the nation back then. The young people talked about the prices and the relative risks of buying new versus used guns. The problem with a used gun was that you didn't know if it had "bodies" attached to it. In other words, the gun could very easily have been used in one or more murders, and if you were then caught with it there was a good chance you would end up being accused of committing this murder(s).

I didn't have to be told by experts that the new marketing strategy by the handgun manufacturers had been a huge success. My young people told me. They helped to open my eyes to how widespread guns are among young people in poor communities—whether bought, bartered, swapped, loaned, or taken from other young people. The handgun generation has already given way to the Uzi generation. Unless we act now, what's next?

If there is a greater threat to the internal security of this country than the current violence, I don't know what it is. The good news is that policy-makers and politicians know that we must do something. The bad news is that what they plan to do won't work.

Chapter Eighteen

•

Broken Strategies

There seems to be a prevailing view in this country that the reason crime and violence are out of hand is that the country has gone "soft on crime." The belief is based in the notion that the "liberal sixties" and our movement toward greater civil rights and protection of individual legal rights loosened society's reins on deviant behavior, and so increasingly allowed the "criminal element" to get away with breaking the law.

From this point of view, the cure for the current crisis is to get tough on crime—meaning more mandatory sentencing, longer jail terms, more arrests. This way, it is assumed, the criminals will get the message, that in the criminal underworld the discussion will go like this. "You know Chuck? He got caught robbing an old lady and got thirty years. And Charles, he got caught breaking into a house and they gave him twenty years. He'll be an old man when he gets out. They're catching everyone and giving them big time. I'm gonna stop robbing. I'm gonna put my gun up and start looking for work tomorrow. Crime just doesn't pay anymore!"

When you see the problems of crime and violence in these simplistic terms, you begin to develop solutions that are also simplistic. In the fall of 1993 Congress began debate on the Crime Bill. The country had finally had enough, and suddenly—even while there seemed to be no money for other services—billions of dollars ($32 billion by the time it was passed) were found for the new bill. And what did the Crime Bill propose we do with all of these dollars? Hire a hundred thousand more police, build more prisons, and create boot camps. Again and again, these bills pass whenever there is a highly visible surge in violence. Again and again, the money is spent on Band-Aids, not meaningful solutions.

The problems with the Crime Bill's basic approach were many. Start with hiring more police. Police have little or no legitimacy in many poor communities. While police corruption might seem like a cyclical problem to the media, the view from the streets is different. The closer you are to the streets, the more evident it is that the police are failing to protect poor people, especially people of color.

The problem is not just that some officers are corrupt and others cover it up while arresting poor young men on a regular basis. It's that the police in poor communities are society's only representatives of justice and fairness, but most police officers who work in the inner cities are not from these neighborhoods. They have no appreciation of the culture or the makeup of the community. They find themselves in a strange environment where the people are often hostile. They don't recognize any sense of community—they see chaos instead—and so often they can't discriminate between one element of the community and another. They end up treating everyone as if they were guilty until proven otherwise. A poor family can't go hire a lawyer to fight for its rights. Most times the closest the poor come to justice in America is the police, and so they often think American justice stinks.

Police officers are given a job to do that is impossible. It doesn't take them long to find out that they are not going to erase crime, so they do the best they can, not really knowing what the overall plan is because there is no overall plan. They end up ruling the streets by intimidation, not because they are respected.

Lack of respect for the police causes young people in poor communities to be extremely cynical regarding illegal activities. In the Harlem precinct that I lived in, the 30th, a huge corruption probe ended in April of

1994, when twelve police officers were arrested for corruption while others were reassigned as punishment for lesser offenses. No one I talked to in Harlem was surprised. We knew that corruption had been rampant for years. As word of the arrests spread, the young drug dealers on the corner just smirked, and I knew my job would be that much harder because their vision of reality, that everyone is out to make a fast buck, was publicly confirmed. In the end, from the street level society looks so corrupt that young people can easily justify "doing what they have to do" to earn money. And this hasn't changed in the twenty-first century, especially as recession forced even more youth into unemployment. It's gotten so bad that, in May of 2010, the *New York Times* reported that city high school students were organizing marches "to push lawmakers to come up with money for summer youth jobs programs as Congress did last year, allocating $1.2 billion for a program for low-income youths." If we listen to them, young people will tell us what they need to keep them safe and off the streets; if we don't listen, hopefully more of them will start organizing and demanding that we act in the way that these New York City students have.

It is truly an irony that the people in these poor communities, people who so desperately need police protection because they are disproportionately the victims of crime in this country, feel they cannot trust the police. So they don't help or support them.

In communities that are very poor there will always be children willing to work the streets for money—no matter how many you arrest, there will always be more. To get to the criminal leadership, those employing these children, the community has to come forward. But as long as the community is worried that the police cannot be trusted, no one will. Everyone on the streets knows a snitch will be killed. If you don't have absolute trust in the police, you'll never tell on anybody, and so people don't.

Young black men in particular are suspicious of the police. They know that they are always in danger of being arrested. I was happy when I no longer looked like a young man because this afforded me a little extra protection—the police were less likely to think of me as a suspect. But I know that I am one of the lucky ones in never having had to go to jail.

Black men and especially young black men have a troubled relationship with the police. My male friends and I talk about it from time to time. As our children have gotten older we've become concerned that they might not have learned the lessons we did when we were growing up. To a great degree money can protect you from police harassment and from being arrested for no cause, so our children have had very little of the antagonistic conflict with the police that many of us learned to accept as an everyday occurrence when we were young. We also learned that no matter what the truth, judges tended to take the police officer's word in court. Even on that rare occasion when a young black man was found innocent, he still usually had to spend a night in jail. The police officer, if he just wanted to "teach you a lesson," would simply "detain" you for hours while you'd be cursed, threatened, and intimidated in the precinct house. And the poorer you were, the more certain the police were that they could act with impunity.

In poor communities the police simply tend to be more hostile, aggressive, and racist than in middle-class communities. Many middle-class people in America have a hard time understanding why poor communities don't necessarily see police as helpful in deterring crime, because in middle-class communities police tend to act differently. The friendly officer who has a citizen's best interest at heart in one community is the hostile officer who shows nothing but disrespect in the other. When you have a mostly white police force in a community of color, the problem gets ten times worse.

So the solution of adding more of the same kind of policing to poor communities won't work. While I am a believer in community policing, if the officer doesn't understand and like the residents in the community where he or she is assigned, I don't see this strategy making a real difference. If we are going to hire more police, we should hire officers that come from the communities in which they work, and we should make sure that a significant number of those hired are minority officers.

In order to reduce crime and violence for real, police must do more than lock up more people for longer periods of time. The sense in America that we have been soft on crime is not borne out by the facts. Indeed, our country incarcerates more people in terms of percentage of our population than any other, even more so in the new century, when we now throw one out of every one hundred adults behind bars. And black men have been incarcerated at an all-time high over the last three decades. A large portion of this rush to lock people up and throw away the key came from our so-called "war on drugs." Writing in the *New York Times* in 2008, journalist Adam Liptak reported, "In 1980, there were about 40,000 people in American jails and prisons for drug crimes. These days, there are almost 500,000." These arrests have impacted black youth more than any other in this country. Nationally, more than 1 million students drop out of high school every year, and 60 percent of young black men who drop out land in prison by their thirties. Incarcerating them can cost better than forty thousand dollars a year. We spend a fraction of that on each of our children in the HCZ, and we make sure they all go on to college.

The reality is this: we pay more to incarcerate kids across this nation than we do to educate them. Can we afford to lock up even more? Cities around this country are coming face to face with municipal budgets that can't provide sufficient funds for schools, roads, and social services. One of the primary reasons these cities are so strapped is that so much of their revenue is being spent on criminal justice. And what have we gotten for all that money? As I told Stephen Colbert the first time I appeared on his show, *The Colbert Report,* America is not number one or even in the top fifteen when it comes to reading, math, and English. We're number one in locking up children. Are our streets safer as a result? The answer is no. While we have foolishly invested our precious resources in a criminal justice approach to solving our crime problem, we have nothing to show for it except poorer schools, poorer services for youth, and more people on the streets unemployable because they have a criminal record. Instead of educating and investing in young people to help them grow up and eventually give back to this great country, we have a crisis of violent youth on our streets that we pretend can be solved by a strategy that has already failed.

While we should all be vitally concerned about the violence occurring around us, we must be smart enough to resist the temptation to look for simplistic solutions that will not work. Violence is a complex problem, and we must be ready to commit the intellectual and financial resources necessary to come up with true solutions. It will not be easy, but there are some things that are already working.

Chapter Nineteen

●

Beacon Schools

It was 1990, and Joe Stewart, Shawn Dove, and I were walking the streets of Harlem looking for a site for our new Beacon school. The Beacon Schools program, developed by Rheedlen's former head, Richard Murphy (in 1990, commissioner of the New York City Department of Youth Services), involved redesigning schools to become multiservice centers to be open days and evenings, 7 days a week, 365 days a year. I thought the choice of school was as important as what we would later do there. We wanted one that would be representative of any public school in any low-income neighborhood in America.

We had already rejected several. Most of the schools in Harlem needed some or all of the supportive services we would bring to them, but some schools were more needy than others. One we rejected because it was already rich in resources, another because the school was isolated, not surrounded by a community. After looking for weeks, Joe and Shawn came to me excited.

Shawn began the conversation. "Geoff, I think we found our school. It's an elementary school on 144th Street and it looks perfect. It's an old building on a block that's struggling to make it. There are several abandoned buildings on the block and people selling drugs on both corners." Joe continued without missing a beat. "It's surrounded by a housing project and has the highest number of children living in temporary housing in Harlem. There are junkies sitting on an old couch right outside, nodding while children come and go. Geoff, I think this is it."

We wanted to do more than just provide services in a school; we wanted to begin to rebuild the community, to help a struggling community find its feet and change its direction from despair to hope. I sent Joe and Shawn back to do a door-to-door survey of the surrounding neighborhood. They reported that scant services existed in any of the areas we deemed important: education, employment, recreation, drug counseling, mental health, cultural activities. There were no such services on weekends or after 6:00 P.M. It had been decided that I would visit the school with Joe and Shawn, and so here we were.

As we turned the corner onto 144th Street from Adam Clayton Boulevard and walked toward Frederick Douglass Boulevard, I could see why Joe and Shawn thought this school was it. At first glance I saw the extreme poverty and felt the sense of desolation. The young men and teenagers hanging on the corner looked at us with open hostility, knowing that three black men with coats and ties had to be a threat of some kind. They thought we were either cops or maybe real estate speculators coming to displace more people from their neighborhood. The only adults visible were sitting not ten yards from the entrance to the school, drinking beer and wine and not even bothering to hide the open bottles. They too looked at us with suspicion. It was clear that to everyone on the block we were a momentary interruption in their existence, people in ties just passing through. This was a block that people who could afford to had long since fled, a block you can find in any city in America.

As I stood on 144th Street and looked closer I could see other things. Things not so apparent to the untrained eye. Some buildings were dirty and their sidewalks garbage-strewn, but a couple had their front stoops swept neat and clean. Several older people chatted for a few minutes and then hurried to their apartment buildings. The school, named Countee Cullen after the famous Harlem poet and playwright, took up half the block. The three of us just stood there and looked at it, each one of us lost in our own thoughts about how we could help transform the community through this school.

When we walked back down the block I saw a woman nodding from heroin on the old couch. Joe's eyes caught mine and his eyebrows went up as if to say, "See what I told you? Nodding right here in the open next to the entrance of the school!" I smiled to myself and thought, "Yep, this is it. I think we found our school."

The week before we were to open the Countee Cullen Community Center at that school, Joe and Shawn asked to see me.

"They killed a young man right next to the entrance of the school last night," Shawn reported. "Shot him dead." My heart skipped a beat. I looked at both of them very closely. I knew Joe's experience getting shot himself had not dampened his enthusiasm for our kind of work, but was this an omen? We three had all discussed the danger of running a program that was to be open nights and weekends and available to all free of cost. There was bound to be a risk of serious injury, but we had thought we'd have some time to acclimate ourselves at Countee Cullen before confronting the reality of life and death in inner-city America.

"How are you guys doing?" I asked, almost afraid of the answer.

"Well, I'm all right. I'm ready to go," Shawn answered.

"This is the work. This just shows us we picked the right place," Joe chimed in.

I tried to hide my feelings and had to turn away quickly to regain my composure as my eyes welled up with tears. They knew and I knew that they were prepared to do whatever it took to change this community. Yep, we had chosen the right school. But Joe and Shawn and people like them are the true heroes in this country. Working out of the glare of public attention, often anonymously, putting their lives on the line for poor children.

Since the Countee Cullen Community Center's creation in 1991, I have prayed to God every night to keep my people, my staff, the children, and their families safe. Today, the center, one of the first Beacons in New York City, has become a national model program. You wouldn't even recognize the location as the same place I visited with Joe and Shawn. The biggest difference is how many people gather there now. The center now serves hundreds upon hundreds of children and adults. It even has a summer camp. One thing hasn't changed. Our motto still is "whatever it takes," as in whatever it takes to meet the needs of the surrounding community, and we will not accept failure under any circumstances.

Chapter Twenty

●

The Community Concept

When dealing with the issue of young people and violence in our country, it's clear that we can't separate violence from all of the other problems that plague our youth: educational failure, teenage pregnancy, drug and alcohol abuse, lack of employment, crime, AIDS . . . the list goes on and on. And we know we cannot design a few small demonstration projects and expect to have any real impact on any of these issues. We can't expect to make a difference unless we are willing to talk about comprehensive services for massive numbers of children *and* their families. The Beacon Schools program is one model to accomplish this.

The Beacon Schools concept is fairly simple; the most complicated part was getting government to make the investment to start the program. It was the mayor of New York City, David N. Dinkins, who decided in 1991 to turn a crime prevention plan from one that merely hired more police to one that invested in children. Story has it that Mayor Dinkins had to decide between a prison barge to handle the overcrowding in city jails or Beacon Schools. He chose Beacons. Through all the administrations that followed,

I have managed to hold on to that one simple ideal: rather than build more prisons, build positive and healthy spaces for children and communities.

People often ask me if "a Beacon" must be a school. The answer is no. The Beacon sites are places that combine comprehensive services with activities based on a youth development model. Schools are a natural place to house Beacon programs because, when designed correctly, a Beacon is more than just a bunch of services for children and families; it is a community development strategy. Beacons work on many issues at the same time, and schools are designed to handle the large numbers of people that must be involved in order to rebuild communities. We have realized that you cannot save children without saving families, and you cannot save families without rebuilding communities. That's not just the belief behind our Beacon programs, but the founding principle at the heart of the entire Harlem Children's Zone.

The other issue to consider when creating these kinds of programs is that schools exist in almost every community, and in almost every poor community they are closed or underutilized after 3:00 P.M. In New York City we argued that we the taxpayers paid for these buildings, so why shouldn't they be used by the whole community during and after school hours?

Our organization has worked in schools for more than two decades, and we don't underestimate the difficulty of sharing space and dealing with school bureaucracies. (Outsiders are not always wanted in schools, especially in schools that are failing, where there is often a "circle the wagons" mentality.) Still, schools offer us our best hope of reaching the millions of children in desperate need of after-school, evening, and weekend activities.

It seems everyone has come to the conclusion that you can't rebuild a community without community residents being "at the table." Those of us who work with Beacon Schools know that the residents must be involved at the beginning to help formulate and develop plans. This is not an easy process. Most people in poor communities are very distrustful of outsiders, especially those who claim to want to help them but don't want to share real power. Many think of outside agencies and "do-gooders" as carpetbaggers, there to make a quick buck off their misery and then move on.

From day one, we decided that even after we had developed a great program inside our Beacon school we needed the people who lived in the buildings surrounding the school to know that something special was happening. We knew that in Central Harlem, as in communities all across this country, good people were so afraid of crime that they came home and locked their doors and barred their windows. The sense of trust that exists when people know their neighbors, others who live on the block, and the children in the community had been severely damaged. We knew that the truth of the matter was that most people in the neighborhood were good people, not involved in crime, drugs, or anything else illegal. They just happened to be poor, and often scared. It was the fear that had run them inside (stray bullets have killed many an innocent bystander in New York City). We knew that we had to get them back outside and talking with one another.

What we did was to have several performances by a theatre company right on the block. People heard the laughing and music and began to open their windows to find out what was happening. Slowly they began to come downstairs, and when they did they saw a first-rate theatre group. People naturally started to talk to one another and to get to know others who lived on the block. This was the beginning of a strategy to get the community's residents to meet one another and to become aware of what we were trying to do.

Another key component to involving the community was the creation of a block association on 144th Street. We encouraged the adults to come together and decide what they wanted for the children on their block, and we said we'd help them to do what *they* wanted. They decided they wanted a "play street." You have to be a New Yorker to understand why this is an extremely difficult thing to get accomplished in New York City. It's not because of the city permit required, or the community board approval process. It's because of parking. New Yorkers are required to move their cars to alternate sides of the street on alternate days so the streets can be cleaned. This requires everyone to double-park and is a huge hassle. A play street means that no cars are allowed on the block at all from 8:00 A.M. until 4:00 P.M., which means that not only do you have to worry about double-parking, but you have to do it on someone else's block.

There was a huge debate about the play street on 144th Street. People with cars were upset. Where were they supposed to park? What if someone broke into their cars while they were on some other block? Others pleaded for the children, asking car owners to make the sacrifice for them. In the end the block decided to open the play street. Now in the summer when you look down 144th Street you can see children engaged in all kinds of activities—and a smug look on the faces of adults who know they are doing the right thing for the children even if it hurts.

One critical strategy of the Beacon Schools program is providing activities designed for adolescents during the late evenings and weekends. Typically, poor communities like Harlem offer few services to children after school hours; where services are offered, they usually end by 6:00 P.M. and are hardly ever available on weekends. When we surveyed what was available for children in our Central Harlem neighborhood we identified approximately five thousand children who needed late-evening activities on the weekend. If we didn't include the children we were serving at our Beacon school, we could only find services elsewhere for approximately fifty of those children. If we expect our young people to engage in positive activities, we must provide them the places and the structure to do so. Leaving thousands of them on street corners with nothing to do only invites trouble.

Since its creation, our Beacon school was designed to provide activities beyond those for children and adolescents. We discovered long ago that we cannot save children without making just as strong an effort to help their parents. Our Beacon offers a range of programs for adults, including education classes, support groups, aerobics, African dance, and targeted workshops in areas that parents select. We also have trained social workers on site to provide more intensive counseling and referral if parents need it.

One of the unanticipated results of having so many parents involved in our Beacon program is that it has reduced the level of violence in the school itself. When we began to think about it, this made sense. Young people are less likely to act violently in a setting where their mother, or their friend's mother, might be. As the Countee Cullen Community Center involved more and more of the community, adults and children, the school and the center took on more of the values of the larger community and fewer of the values of the adolescents in that community. Knowing that someone's mother could be walking down the hallway or sitting in a nearby classroom, the children became less likely to yell curses or engage in violent behavior.

The Beacon program at Countee Cullen is designed to help rebuild the

Central Harlem community that surrounds it, but it is also designed to help support the education of the young children who attend the elementary school. Our staff have become directly involved in working with these students. They have helped with counseling, instruction, and bridging the gap between school and home. It is often obvious that a child having a difficult time in school has a problem at home. Schools today don't have the ability or training to go to a child's home when a parent will not come to the school. I'm proud to say that our staff will make that home visit and work with that parent and the entire family. In this way the home and school connection can be strengthened and teachers can get support dealing with even the most difficult children.

Safety is so important when you have a large building like Countee Cullen, with its five floors, one that stays open so many hours, especially late evenings. We have a security force that makes sure the message received at the front door is that we expect good manners, and no violence. The young men and women who make up our security team really like the children and don't try to intimidate them. When there's a problem they try to reason, but they are firm. They don't believe in using force or bad language, or in bending the rules, which get enforced fairly by all the members of the team. If there is a problem, members of the security team use their walkie-talkies to converge on the problem site and defuse the situation before it can get out of hand. If someone is really aggressive and refuses to obey the security team, the police are called to expel that person. The police, as we've seen, are not well loved by young people in Harlem, so we use them sparingly. We have had to call the police only a few times in the years we have been open, and we maintain a good relationship with our community police officer.

After decades of hard and good work, our Beacon school has had its desired effect. Over the course of a week more than a thousand children and adults come to our programs. The whole community benefits from so many people just being outside, walking in the community, on their way to or from healthy activities. The teenagers have begun to exert real control over their lives. For example, they decided that a huge billboard on 144th Street, one that was right across from the school and had advertised cigarettes or alcohol their whole lives, needed to be changed. Our Teen Youth

Council fought to have the usual ad replaced by one for the United Negro College Fund. Now, instead of the children on that block and in the school seeing a compelling reason to drink or smoke, they see a picture of Martin Luther King Jr. urging them to go to college.

The Teen Youth Council has also decided to improve the physical conditions on 144th Street. They have regularly cleaned the block and painted over graffiti, and one winter they got trees planted up and down the whole block. They've led hunger drives for the homeless, clothing drives for poor people, voter registration drives aimed at nonvoters, and antiviolence demonstrations to get the message out that, in a world where they have felt their odds of surviving to adulthood to be shrinking, they want the opportunity to grow up.

There are many exciting things occurring at Countee Cullen. Even better, we have copied that success in the Booker T. Washington Beacon, which even helps young people who are no longer in school achieve their high-school equivalency degree, and the HCZ Community Center, which has expanded to offer programs within two nearby housing projects and offers after-school enrichment to our Promise Academy students. The HCZ center even provides an annual Thanksgiving dinner to the surrounding community.

The three Promise Academy charter schools, which began in 2004, were created as a partnership with the Harlem Children's Zone. We call each school a "Promise Academy" because we promise our families that their children are going to get into college. The goal for all of these schools is to run from kindergarten through twelfth grade. But we try to start even sooner, with Baby College, a series of workshops we offer to hundreds of parents in the community who are expecting or already have young ones. We stay with our children until we get them into college, and then we help them graduate from college so that these kids can be competitive in America.

Many of the children in our Promise Academy schools spend ten or more hours a day under the watchful guidance of talented, loving staff. In addition to all of our academic and enrichment programs, these kids receive healthy and freshly prepared meals, plus medical, dental, and mental-health services. On another track, we work to support public schools within our ninety-seven-block Central Harlem zone. Everything is free and these children deserve all of it. Not only do they deserve it, but we are convinced that, to borrow President Bill Clinton's words about investing in the HCZ, "you know you will get a high rate of return."

The HCZ began as a one-block pilot project in the 1990s. Back then I used to keep a list of the names of hundreds of children who were waiting to get into our small program, with its limited number of openings. I would see in the eyes of mothers and fathers the fear and clear understanding that the system is designed so that their kids were probably not going to make it if they didn't get in.

That list used to drive me crazy. I would stare at it and wonder why it was that these children wouldn't get an equal chance to make it as the ones in our program. Why not push the borders of our zone to include these kids and their families. Why not? To quote President Barack Obama, "Why not?" is "the final question about poverty in America. It's the hopeful one that Bobby Kennedy was also famous for asking. Why not? It leaves the cynics without an answer, and it calls on the rest of us to get to work."

As we got to work reweaving the social fabric of Harlem, a once vibrant community torn apart by crime, drugs, and endemic poverty, we held before us two fundamental principles: help kids in a sustained way, starting as early in their lives as possible, and create a critical mass of adults around them who understand what it takes to help children succeed. We are determined that our parents are going to give their children something better than generational poverty.

You know you are on the right track when so many people come from near and far to observe what you are doing. These visitors often ask me how the students feel about the signs on the school walls that read: "Failure is not an option." They are surprised to hear that the signs are really for the staff. We've had a lot more visitors in recent years, after President Obama saw that what we were doing here in Harlem works and decided that, as part of his plan to combat urban poverty, he will replicate the Harlem Children's Zone in twenty cities across the country. Why not?

Chapter Twenty-one

●

One Shot

It had been a long day and it looked like it would be a long night. I had started the day by boarding a plane at 7:00 A.M. to go to Chicago to speak at a conference entitled "Children in a Violent America." The last few months had been murder for me. I was starting to feel like airports were my second home, and my days were starting earlier and ending later. The job has always required some seven-day work weeks, but it had been harder and harder to take even one day off.

I didn't want to go on what was my second trip to Chicago in one week. At the time, I had been doing a lot of traveling, speaking to groups around the country on the work we were doing. I couldn't respond to all the important requests—as it was I had been away from the center more than I wanted to be. But Chicago I couldn't refuse.

Chicago was a city under siege. It had constantly been in the news because of the severity of its violence and crime. There were proposals to gain blanket permission to search the apartments in its notorious housing projects, and even to tear down some of those projects as an admission that

147

they just weren't made to work. I thought of the children trapped in the projects in Chicago and identified with how abandoned and isolated they must feel.

I remember all too well feeling that way myself. It was the night of my junior high school graduation party, around 9:00 P.M., and I was leaving my building on Union Avenue. I was walking with two girls who were in my class and were also going to the graduation. As we came out of my building there was a man lying on the ground across the street crying out for help. The man standing over him was kicking him in the head viciously, over and over again. The girls, who lived in a better part of the Bronx, wanted to run, to yell for help, to do *something*. I remember telling them, "This is Union Avenue, ain't no cops coming here. If we get involved I'm just going to end up fighting that man, and Mike and the guys will come to help me and we'll end up kicking him the same way he's kicking that other guy. Forget about it. That's just the way it is around here. Let's go." And we walked on down the block trying to pretend all was OK, but that was hard to do with the man's pleading and the thud of the shoe over and over again in our ears. I remember thinking later that night that I had to get away from Union Avenue. Nobody cared what happened to you in places like this. You could be killed on the streets and people would just step over your body and keep walking. I felt abandoned by all the world, left to fend for myself.

The Chicago talk went well, but I couldn't shake the feeling that too many people still didn't realize how serious the crisis is for children in this country, and that those who did realize it didn't know what to do about it. That made the visit we were expecting that evening from Attorney General Janet Reno to our Beacon school even more important. The call had come earlier in the week: Janet Reno wanted to come in the evening to look at the kinds of programs that could be offered to keep young people engaged in positive activities during the late hours. She was scheduled to arrive at 10:00 P.M. that same Thursday I'd be speaking in Chicago.

I had met the attorney general just two weeks earlier, when two of our children from the Beacon school and I were giving testimony on child violence to the Senate Judiciary Committee. The children made a real impression on the senators. One young boy in particular, only eleven years old, told the poignant and revealing story of his young life, of how he had seen two people killed in his Central Harlem neighborhood and how gunshots were fairly common. He had eventually stopped going to school and with two older boys robbed other children of their money and sometimes clothing. He explained how one of our center's workers had changed his life, and said that now he hardly ever missed school and that his grades were much improved. He was asked how the worker had reached him. His answer: "He made a deal with me. If I went to school and did well he would take me to a fancy restaurant once a week." When asked what kind of fancy restaurant he was taken to, he answered, "Ahhh, you know—Wendy's, that kind." The senators and audience couldn't help but laugh. A child's life turned around, the cost: time with a caring adult and a couple of hamburgers.

The Janet Reno visit went well. She seemed to enjoy the young people and they seemed to genuinely like her. The most touching moment for me came when she was presented with flowers and a basketball shirt by a young man we'd spent an inordinate amount of time and energy trying to save. Only sixteen years old, this boy used the middle name of a notorious mob kingpin. His ambition was clear; he wanted to be a gangster. I had been involved by Joe and Shawn on several occasions because of the young man's propensity for violence, and I was as surprised as pleased when Shawn told me that this boy had been elected vice president of the Teen Youth Council and was in the process of writing a book. The Countee Cullen Community Center had turned this young man around. He is a gifted poet and now spends his energy writing poems instead of cursing and fighting the way he used to.

Still, I was stunned when he handed Janet Reno the flowers and the shirt that the Teen Youth Council had brought for her, and then hugged her. She hugged him back, unaware that this was a person who only a short time before had considered all law enforcement people as the enemy. The young man was really touched that the attorney general had come to Harlem.

We had decided that after Janet Reno had spent some time talking about her support for programs that deter young people from jail, and taking questions, we'd ask her if she'd shoot a basket or two in the gym, where about eighty young people were participating in a late-night basketball tournament. She agreed. She dribbled to the basket, shot, and missed. She shot again, missed. After her sixth or seventh attempt she stopped. All the young people in the gym clapped, but you could tell they wanted her to make a shot. I don't know what it was, but they needed her to make a shot.

She was asked to try again. I was worried because it was already 11:00 P.M. and she was obviously tired from a long day on the road. She picked up the basketball and shot again, and missed. She shot five, six, seven times and missed them all. The whole gymnasium groaned as one ball rolled around the rim two times and then came out of the basket. She shot again and the ball hit the backboard, looked as if it was going to come out, and then went in. The young people screamed their approval. You would have thought the Knicks had just won the championship.

I thought then about our children at our Beacon school in Harlem. Many have so little, but they have so much to give. They really wanted Janet Reno to hit a basket. They were patient and supportive while she missed shots from right underneath. Any one of them could have made those shots easily, yet they didn't laugh or ridicule her; they knew in time she would get it done. And when she finally made the basket, they cheered her. How proud I was of our young people. I couldn't help think that this is what we are trying to do at our Beacon school—believe in our children, support them, be patient with them, knowing that eventually they will succeed. And then cheering with all our heart when they do.

Chapter Twenty-two

•

Peacemakers

The Beacon programs are good first steps in connecting children to caring adults and increasing the likelihood that children will interact peaceably. But I felt that we needed to go further. Ever more violent codes of conduct still ruled the streets in our neighborhood, and young people were still at a very high risk of being killed for little or no reason. We had to become more aggressive in making peace fashionable, and I had an idea. I had been toying with it for some time, but it was my good friend Rasuli Lewis who helped me put it all together.

At the time, Rasuli was on the Rheedlen staff and coordinating our work with the national Black Community Crusade for Children. We were discussing his dream of going to the United Nations as an ambassador for children, and how our children need to learn the same skills that are taught to U.N. peacekeepers. It hit us both at the same time: that's exactly what young people need to know, how the experts make peace. There is a war raging in our inner cities across this country, and our children are the main combatants. We are fighting wars overseas and our children are being killed in larger numbers right here in the United States. Here in New York City, police wear bulletproof vests, were recently issued nine-millimeter handguns, travel in twos, and are always in touch with their command posts by walkie-talkie. Yet when you look at the data about deaths from firearms, it's more dangerous to be a four year old in America than to be a law enforcement officer. And still the debate is focused too much on how to support the police, not enough on how to support children—children who die far more frequently than the police, children who have no training in survival, no bulletproof vests, no "backup." Where do children go for training in survival and in making peace?

Rasuli and I knew we had to create such a place. We began to design the Peacemakers program, which has at its core teaching children the same negotiating skills others use to make peace in hostile territory. We figured our children stand more of a chance of being killed on 144th Street than do members of U.N. peacekeeping forces in war-ravaged countries—and that we ought to be giving them some real skills in making peace.

Rasuli and I understood that there have always been children who acted as peacemakers. When two children are ready to fight, another often steps forward to say, "C'mon, you two, don't fight. It ain't worth it." Or one child might say another is her sister or cousin to prevent the bullying of that child. But making peace has always included the risk that the peacemaker may become the target of the aggression. In my time that meant you might end up in a fight. Today it means you might end up getting shot. Today, children take a much greater risk when playing the role of peacemaker, and we must do that much more to prepare them and support them.

One of the key components of our Peacemakers program is involving the children themselves in designing effective antiviolence strategies. The peacemakers are trained not only in conflict resolution but also in how to create "safety plans." Safety plans are a crucial element to making peace. These plans are necessary because adults often pay little or no attention to where violence is likely to occur in schools or after-school programs. But children know. Children know where fights happen, and why those places are chosen. While this information is common knowledge among children, adults never ask *them* how to reduce or prevent violence. We go about hiring security guards or bringing in metal detectors, with no thought that children can tell us much of what we need to know about violence reduction.

Children don't talk to adults about violence because being a snitch is so frowned upon by other children, and because it is just too risky to trust adults to keep information confidential. Many children at one time or another have confided in an adult only to have the adult, who thinks he or she knows best, break that confidence. Once the confidence is broken, children find it difficult to trust adults again. I know from experience the perils of trusting an adult.

It was 1966 and I was in the eighth grade at John Dwyer Junior High School 133. I was at that school even though it was not my neighborhood school because it had an SP ("special progress") class. I had qualified for this accelerated junior high school program because of my reading and math test scores in elementary school. I was happy to be going to a "good" class but sorry that I would be leaving all of "my boys" on Union Avenue, who would go to another junior high school. Even though John Dwyer was only eight blocks from my apartment building, it was in a section of the South Bronx that I didn't know, and I had no friends who lived there.

J.H.S. 133, like so many other large public schools in New York City, had a strict tracking system. There were two special progress classes, then the classes ran from 7-1 through 7-21—the higher the number, the lower the expectation. There was no expectation that college was an option for anyone "below" 7-2. Children who were in classes below 7-6 knew they were just marking time, that no one expected them to go anywhere. This well-understood hierarchy posed a particular problem for me, because there was among the children an assumed inverse relationship between intelligence and ability to fight. Everyone assumed that those in the "smartest" classes couldn't fight and those in the "dumbest" classes could.

People often say to me that there seems to be a bias against poor minority children who do well in school, that they are actually punished by other kids for being "smart." This is true in many cases. The smart children are perceived as weak, and weakness is something that is often punished in poor communities. The best way I can describe it is that many children feel that their lives are so harsh, so uncertain, that when they see a child doing well in school and adopting middle-class norms and attitudes it triggers the reaction "You think I'm going to suffer and live a life of fear, fear for my future, fear for my safety, fear for my very existence, and you're gonna just waltz through life and make it out of here? No way. You ought to feel pain and fear and doubt just like the rest of us." And so they target those kids to make sure they don't escape without "paying their dues."

The "dues" I remember were a constant stream of petty humiliations—others cutting in front of you in the lunch line, making jokes about you out loud, taking your lunch money. In the street terminology of the 1960s you were a "punk," and for those of us on Union Avenue this was a fate worse than death. It didn't take long for me to realize I had to show the others in the school that I wasn't to be treated like my peers in the special progress classes. I wasn't in school more than two weeks before I made it clear to one of the "bad" boys in the school that his challenge to me wasn't going to go unanswered—I was ready to fight. We agreed to meet right after school, down the block.

I was anxious all that day, dreading the fight, not because I was scared of the boy, him I was sure I could beat. It was his friends I was worried about. I needed someone to watch my back so I wouldn't get jumped. I found only one person willing to go with me, my best friend at the school, a boy in my class named William. We went to the designated place after school and I breathed a sigh of relief when neither the "bad" boy nor his friends were there. He'd been bluffing. He really didn't want to fight and thought he was in safe territory challenging a "bookworm." I had no further problems with kids wanting to fight me at Dwyer. When it comes to violence the word travels quickly in schools.

William, a brilliant student from a middle-class home and no street fighter, wasn't so lucky. A year later, when we were eighth-graders, I was playing handball in the handball court at lunchtime. I heard the yelling and screaming that meant someone was fighting, but the game was tough and I had my opponents on the run, so I paid no attention. It was one of my classmates who ran to the chain-link fence that enclosed the handball court and yelled, "It's William, Geoff! He's fighting Billy!" Billy was one of the toughest kids in the school. He was on the basketball team and I knew he had plenty of tough friends. I sprinted for the crowd of yelling kids that surrounded the combatants.

By the time I'd fought my way through the mob of kids the fight was mostly over. William had suffered a nasty cut on his upper lip. Billy's friends were yelling encouragement. "Kick his ass, Billy! C'mon, kick his ass." Poor William, looking frightened, hurt, and alone, was doing his best. I yelled as loud as I could, "C'mon, William, fuck him up. C'mon, git him." Billy's friends turned to see who this lone voice was, rooting against their boy. They were not happy to see me. I didn't care; William was my boy and I wouldn't let him suffer alone. I knew fighting was as much emotional as physical. Few fighters could keep their confidence after sustaining a serious cut. Blood distracted and sapped the will; only the toughest street fighters could suffer a cut like William's and come back to win the fight. And William, as I've said, was not a tough street fighter.

The school bell signaled the end of the fight. Billy started talking trash that he was going to get William again, looked at me, and said, "I'm gonna get you too." I answered immediately. "You ain't doing shit to me." André, one of Billy's best friends and one of the most feared boys in the school, said, "What you gonna do? You want some static?" While I was willing to take on Billy, André was another matter. I tried to defuse the situation. "I ain't got no beef with you, André, but ain't nobody gonna mess with my boy." Billy chimed in. "We'll fuck all of you up. You, that sissy I just fucked up, and all the rest of you eggheads." The bell rang again, this time it was the late bell. André pulled at Billy and said, "Let's get them after school. We'll see how smart they are then." And the group left to go into the school.

William was in pretty bad shape. After Billy had gotten in the first punch and busted William's lip early in the fight it had been tough enough to fight the rest of the time with kids pointing at him and laughing. He was in no condition to have a second fight after school. I tried to rally the other boys in our class to stand up to André, Billy, and their gang, but had no success. None of them wanted anything to do with taking on that bunch. So William and I were left alone to figure out what to do. I had no doubt that Billy's bunch would be waiting for us after school. We'd be outnumbered and would probably take a pretty serious beating. I knew that I would then have to get "my boys" from

Union Avenue and come back for revenge. Then they would get their boys from wherever they lived to get *their* revenge, and we would be at war.

William and I decided on a tricky strategy, one filled with serious risks but the only way I knew to get out of the trap. We decided to go to the principal of the school and tell all. We would ask him to intervene and warn Billy and André not to jump us. And we'd ask him to pretend he'd heard the news from a teacher who'd overheard some kids talking about the impending fight; that way the other boys would never suspect us of snitching on them. We snuck to the principal's office, making sure no one saw us go in. We explained our dilemma, swearing the principal to secrecy. He agreed that he would be discreet and handle this matter sensitively. He asked us to wait in the anteroom next to his office. We waited.

After about fifteen minutes, to our horror, who did we see coming into the office but Billy, André, and three other boys who were part of their group. They walked by us and their looks told the whole story. We were dead. I couldn't believe the principal had violated our trust. We walked in a state of shock back to our classroom. There was no way out of the trap now.

There is no doubt in my mind that if I'd had access to a gun I would have been prepared to use it that day. There was no way I was willing to desert William, and he was in no shape either psychologically or physically to fight again. I knew that if we both "went for bad" there was a good chance that the fight would be brutal but brief. But the condition William was in meant we would have to try to "cop a plea," and that would probably lead us to being taken for punks and attacked even more viciously.

The confrontation happened before we left school. We were hoping we could escape early, before the three o'clock bell. It wasn't until we had almost reached the door leading to the street that we saw them. William and I both stopped for a fraction of a second, thinking that if they hadn't seen us we would turn around and head in the opposite direction, but it was too late. André was the one who called us. "Oh, there goes the snitches who ratted us out. You two come here." It was an imperious command, one not to be refused. I knew that the next few minutes would be critical. My mind went into what by now was an old familiar place—too late now to do anything but show no fear and prepare for war.

I looked André right in his eyes. I tried to dominate him with my stare.

It wasn't a threatening stare, but it was a challenge. Where he expected to see fear he saw none. My hands slid into my pockets as I "bopped" over to where they were standing. I knew that putting my hands in my pockets was potentially suicidal, as I would never be able to get them out in time to defend myself, but by doing so I was making André deal with my behavior: was I nuts or just so unafraid, so confident, that I knew he wouldn't attack me?

This wasn't the first time I had used this gambit. When I was in the seventh grade some boys from Home Street and I got into a verbal altercation over a basketball game. I had fought Roy, the ringleader of the Home Street boys, some time ago and had won the "fair one." On this day I dismissed their command to get off the court as they warmed up for a basketball game. I lazily took a few extra shots, looked at them as if they were out of their minds, then sauntered off the court. On the way home with my brother Reuben and my friend Ned, I spotted Roy and two cronies following us. I knew there would be trouble. We turned to face them on Home Street, fifty yards from the safety of Union Avenue. Roy had "popped" an antenna from a car, a deadly weapon that could slice an unprotected face or arm like a razor. "You want to talk that shit now? Huh? What you got to say now?" Roy challenged as he held the antenna in his right hand, preparing to swing it at me. I knew I was the center of their anger. Neither Reuben nor Ned had done anything to them—they just happened to be with me. As I sized up the situation I realized that Roy was too far away for me to try to grab him; the antenna was a weapon used to keep an opponent at bay. I made a bold decision, one that would take all my years of street combat training to carry out. I looked Roy in his eyes, put my hands in my pockets, and slouched as if I didn't have a care in the world.

This threw Roy off balance. He wasn't prepared for my reaction. "I'm gonna cut you up," he yelled as he pulled the antenna back to strike. I didn't flinch, just looked at him with a quiet confidence that said, "If you cut me with that antenna you'll pay a price you'll never forget." Again Roy pulled back the antenna and acted as if he was going to hit me. Again I didn't move, just tapped my foot on the ground as if to say, "I dare you." Meanwhile I was reading Roy's face. His confusion was obvious. He was trying to decide what to do. I knew that he would reach the decision to strike me, because not to do so would mean that his "boys" would never respect him again.

Soon I saw the determination to attack in his face. Roy figured he would just pull back and strike me with the antenna. Because I hadn't reacted to his feints, his movements were slow and calculated. As he pulled his arm back for the real attack, I hurled myself forward. His strike was too late, catching me on my back as I grabbed him and began to wrestle him for the antenna. He wrenched free and took off up the block toward the safety of his building. I overturned a garbage can and found what I was looking for, a beer bottle. I smashed the bottle on the curb and had my weapon, a jagged bottle neck that had several sharp points as deadly as any knife.

As Roy sped up the block I took off after him, broken bottle in hand. Luckily, Roy knew I wasn't playing. I meant to fight him until the end. The codes of conduct made it mandatory that if someone pulled a weapon on you, you had to retaliate. If you did not, everyone would think that they could face you down with a weapon. Pulling a weapon was one of the most dangerous things you could do on Union Avenue because it left your opponent no option but to get a weapon himself and avenge the threat. I spent the better part of that night looking for Roy and putting the word out that "Geoff said if he catches Roy he's a dead man." As God would have it I never caught Roy. He probably got the message I was looking for him and prudently kept away from Union Avenue. After a few weeks the incident was forgotten, but the lesson it taught wasn't.

So there I was a year later, facing down André, while he was trying to figure out why I seemed so unafraid of him. Billy, the boy William had fought earlier that day, sensed that William had no fight left in him and was spoiling for battle. I was faced with a complicated situation. André was forced by the laws of the street to support Billy, and because we had snitched he could rightfully insist on fighting us. But I saw just the slightest hesitation in his eyes. A light bulb went off in my head: André remembered. Maybe we were saved if André remembered.

It had happened about six months before. There had been some problems with Mike's girl, and her mother had refused to let Mike come visit now or in the future. Mike's girl was pregnant, and there was no way Mike was going to be denied the right to support his woman and his child-to-be, and now was as good a time as any to make that clear. Mike asked me to come with him to his girl's apartment and explained it would be a dangerous trip. She lived over near Kelly Street, which was way out of our territory. We could be jumped by any number of gangs whose territories we had to cross. It was a great honor for a young boy my age to be asked by an older boy to go on a serious mission like this one. I was terrified to travel into enemy territory. But what could I do? It was a matter of "heart."

Mike asked if I had my knife on me; I told him yes. He was solemn when he gave me my instructions. "Listen, when we get over by Kelly Street there will be a bunch of guys hanging on the stoops. Ignore them. We're bopping. Keep your eyes up and your hand in your pocket on your knife. Don't worry, if they talk shit act like they're not even there. When we get to the stoop there'll be a bunch of guys standing there. They're gonna look you up and down and they won't move. Don't say 'excuse me.' Just follow me. I'm gonna bop right through them. If anything happens, be prepared to fight your way up to the apartment. If they think you're scared they'll fuck with you. You ready?" I shook my head yes, although the truth was I wasn't sure I was ready for something like this.

Mike and I bopped right through the heart of one of the most dangerous sections of the South Bronx. I was amazed by how many young men were hanging on the corners. They all eyed us suspiciously. Some tried to stare us down. It was clear that they knew we were outsiders and they didn't appreciate us bopping through their neighborhood. But Mike could command respect anyplace in the Bronx. None of them challenged us. They could tell by Mike's demeanor that if they did there would be a fight to the death, that he was nobody to mess with.

Once we were deep in enemy territory a group of young men blocked our way. They didn't do so intentionally; they were just hanging on the sidewalk and their group stretched from one side to the other. Mike was clearly going to bop right through them, veering neither right nor left. If they refused to get out of his way, he would force a way clear. If they didn't like it? Well, the fight would be on. I knew this would be a big challenge because we were on Mike's girl's block. People were watching our approach from up the block and it was clear they sensed trouble in the air. I studied the group, looking for a path through them that I could navigate without looking as if I had "punked out." Then I saw him—André. He was standing with the group, drinking a beer, intently watching our approach like all the others were. I knew he didn't recognize me as the boy he knew from the seventh-grade special progress class at J.H.S. 133. I had on my street clothes and looked like a young gangster—hat cocked to the side, jacket collar turned up, sunglasses on, cigarette dangling from my lips.

I couldn't believe our luck. I called out, "André, what's up?" He just looked at me. As I got closer I took off my glasses and he smiled. Then he looked at Mike and looked at me again real hard. It was clear he had a newfound respect for me. He knew who I was, an "egghead," but everyone else had assumed I was a dangerous enemy bent on trouble, the way we bopped on their block. "What you doing around here?" he asked.

"Me and my main man, we got to take care of some business. Somebody fucking with his girl. We got to go straighten it out. You know how it is." André just nodded his head; indeed he did know how it was. He, even more than I, was a product of the street and he knew a "man had to do what a man had to do." We "slapped five" and Mike and I continued on down the street. I was amazed when we came to the girlfriend's building and saw the large number of teenagers hanging on the stoop. Mike just burst through them, bumping a few and hearing the curses that followed. I pushed through the crowd the same way. I had gained a new admiration for Mike. He really was a tough guy and everybody sensed it.

Later that evening, after much yelling and screaming at Mike's girl's house, we passed André on the corner again. I was deep into my "street thing." The sense of power in being with Mike and bopping past hundreds of tough kids without any of them having the heart to challenge us was heady stuff. This time when we passed, André spoke, but I just nodded at him and kept on bopping. We bopped back to the safety of Union Avenue and had a good laugh about how we had "chumped" off all those guys on the street.

Facing André with William by my side, I could tell that he remembered the other Geoff. The one he had seen bop past him and all his boys with some tough dude on some kind of mission. He looked at me. He was unafraid, but he was also as trapped as I was. The code demanded that he support his boy. I seized the opportunity to do some honest fast talking. "André, listen. I didn't want to go and snitch, but my boy don't want to fight no more. Billy beat him in a fair one. But you know how it is; once I thought we were going to be jumped I had to tell. Otherwise I would have had to get my boys and come back and all that shit. I don't want to start no war, not because of a simple fight."

Billy was livid. "Fuck that shit. I'm gonna kick his ass again. You gonna git fucked up too," he said, pointing a finger in my face. I looked at Billy with disdain, hands still in my pockets, and turned back to André. I knew this was André's decision. "We don't want no static." I had copped just enough of a plea to get André off the hook if he wanted off. We were sorry we had told on them, but I was trying not to start a bigger fight. I was insinuating that I could bring my own boys here if I had to. André knew this was not an idle threat. He made his decision. "Geoff's all right, OK? Cool, no problem. Don't do it again. Let's go." And that was it. William and I left school looking over our shoulders just in case it was a setup, but André kept his word, and that particular trouble ended then and there.

However, that day I swore to myself that I would never again trust another teacher or school official when it came to violence. The principal probably thought he had handled the problem just fine; after all, he heard nothing else about it. I knew, though, that I had just barely escaped a serious violent confrontation that might have escalated into a full-scale gang fight. This incident reaffirmed what I had long suspected: when it came to violence, teachers and principals just didn't understand—we were on our own to survive the best way we knew how.

I remember this experience whenever I think that I've come up with some wonderful strategy for dealing with the violence that children face. I try to remember what I once knew, that children are the real experts in violence prevention, that they are the first ones to ask if you really want to know what works and what doesn't. This understanding has informed and guided our development of the Peacemakers program.

We developed this program because we realized that making peace is difficult for children who have grown up fighting enemies real and imagined every day they can remember. The fifty children we selected to train as peacemakers, from Central Harlem and Williamsburg in Brooklyn, were not the best-behaved children, not the ones who received the highest grades in school, but they were strong, courageous, and willing to take risks. And for many of them, trying to make peace in their neighborhood would be a risky venture at best.

I felt compelled to take the peacemakers to Bowdoin College for their week-long initial training session. To Bowdoin, where the quiet and serenity could teach a better lesson about peace than one could ever learn in any classroom. Where the sound of the wind blowing through the summer leaves seemed to whisper, "Child, fear no more. Hear the sound, the sound of peace." I contacted the president of the college, Robert Edwards, and told him of my plan. As I figure it, violence is a problem for all of us if we believe that this is "one nation, indivisible." Colleges like Bowdoin—and other institutions—have to get involved, even if the problem seems distant and removed from them. President Edwards got as excited as I was about the possibility. He promised me the college's full support. And so, in the first week of July 1994, fifty peacemakers aged nine to sixteen, fifteen college interns, and five Rheedlen staff boarded buses heading for Brunswick, Maine.

The week was filled with activities that gave the trainees a chance to decompress and think about making peace. They were taught specific conflict-mediation skills, research skills, community organizing skills, and they started each morning with meditation. But more importantly, they got to experience being away from the front lines of the battlefield. They got to be children again. That week was the beginning of children learning to become leaders in a movement for peace in Harlem and Williamsburg.

In late August, these same peacemakers organized and led a march in Harlem of five hundred children and adults. As they walked the children yelled, "What do we want? *Peace!* When do we want it? *Now!* What do we want? *Peace!* When do we want it? *Now!*" The impact that these children marching for peace had on the adults and youth of Harlem was apparent. People on the streets clapped and chanted with them, while others just stopped, smiled, and nodded their heads yes. The peacemakers had arrived.

* * *

When the Peacemakers program was founded, the expectations for young people in this country seemed to be at a low point. You could tell that simply by reading the label the media had attached to an entire generation. During that time of rising juvenile crime, the media had begun demonizing these youngsters, calling them "super predators." At the HCZ, we see young people another way. We see them as caring and concerned about their friends, families, and communities. We see them as builders, creators, leaders working for a better neighborhood, nation, world. In other words, we see them as part of the solution, not part of the problem. And we are determined to give them the training, tools, and opportunities that help them to be and do their best—in return, we expect a lot from them. And each year we will train more and more peacemakers until there are hundreds and then thousands of children who demand and work toward an end to the violence in their communities and their lives.

Chapter Twenty-three

•

A New Mission

The fact of the matter seems quite simple to me. Either we address the murder and mayhem in our country or we simply won't be able to continue to have the kind of democratic society that we as Americans cherish. Reducing the escalating violence in our country will be a complicated and costly endeavor. If we were fighting an outside enemy that was killing so many of our children we would spare no expense in mounting the effort to subdue that enemy. What happens when the enemy is us? What happens when those American children are mostly black and brown? Do we still have the will to invest the time and resources in saving their lives? The answer must be yes, because the impact and fear of violence has overrun the boundaries of our ghettos and has both its hands firmly around the neck of our whole country.

We lead the Western world in killing our own children. Everyone is saying that terrorism is their number-one priority. But what about those poor children here who will be killed tonight? Tomorrow? Next week? Where is the concern? Where is the outrage? Those who are poor in this country have the weight of poverty and violence and discrimination hanging over their heads, straining to break free and crush them, maybe kill them. There is evil out there. I'm not talking about some mystical, theoretical, hypothetical force. I'm talking about the real thing: pain and suffering, despair, and death. And while you may not yet have been visited by the spectre of death and fear of this new national cancer, just give it time. Sooner or later, unless we act, you will. We all will.

When I was in college, I was absolutely focused on only one thing: how could I improve the outcomes for the poor kids I knew growing up? Every single class I took, I was looking for the answer. Today, there are tens of thousands of talented, smart young people looking for that same answer. It could be a great moment for our country if these young people decide to continue their pursuit for the betterment of society until they've attained that lofty goal.

Our country continues to grapple unsuccessfully with some complex issues. And these complex issues hang over our heads today like a giant, leaden weight suspended by poor logic, faulty reasoning, and a degraded sense of ethics and morality. And I feel this leaden weight will in short order come crashing down on us, crushing all who won't be able to get out of the way.

One of these issues is, of course, poverty. As our country has become the only remaining superpower on the face of the earth, and the richest nation by far, we continue to have rates of poverty in America that shame us. And poverty is not some benign condition that simply means you live a little worse off. Poverty is a killer.

When you battle poverty for a long time, you can grow weary. Yes, even I get a little tired sometimes. When you fight in this battle, if you do it on the front lines, there are things that get to you.

For me it was David Chen Joseph. He was a special person to me. He joined my martial arts class when he was a young boy. Two years later, his mother and father passed away, leaving David Chen and his brothers and sisters with no parent to care for them. The oldest brother dropped out of school and went to work, and we helped as best we could at the Harlem Children's Zone.

I watched David Chen Joseph grow into a fine young man and I adopted David Chen. Not in a formal way, but in the way we do when we tell a child who has no parent "think of me as your father" and he does, and then you begin to think of that child as your own. That's how it was with David Chen and me. David Chen was a boy who went to church and sang in the choir. He was one of our Peacemakers and spent his summers at Bowdoin helping poor children from Harlem learn how to negotiate for peace.

Several years ago they shot and killed my son in a park in New York City. And then there was the question "What can you do?" That was the question all of my children asked of me. Those who loved him wanted that question answered. What could I do? They can kill the best of us: the ones who play by the rules, the ones who were religious, who worked hard and went to college. If they aren't safe, then who is? And in the end, if I couldn't save David Chen, then who could I save? And really, what could I do?

In the end, I couldn't save David Chen. But I gave him what he loved and what he wanted. It wasn't what you might expect. It had been given as a gift from my instructor when I passed my third-degree black belt in tae kwon do: a wonderful black belt with my name and school embroidered in gold thread. We all coveted that belt. It's a silly thing to covet, but I did. The day we buried David Chen, I promoted him to black belt and I gave him my belt, my own. I knew it was a silly thing to do. It was too late for David Chen, but not too late for us. And my children gained hope from the act, and they did not give up and therefore neither did I.

I have this fantasy that plays out in my head. It's something that occasionally happened when I was growing up in the South Bronx. I loved playing basketball, and I was fearless. I wasn't very good, but I could convince my team we could beat anyone. And we would go out, playing all over the Bronx, full of confidence, and invariably lose. My brother John, on the other hand, was a great athlete. He was so good that at thirteen, he was playing with the adults.

Every now and then, this most incredible thing would happen. We younger kids would be sweating on some blacktop in some foreign neighborhood in the South Bronx and losing. Then I would see this wonderful vision: the tall, long, looping stride of my brother John as—having finished playing with the big kids somewhere—he came by to look in on us. And at that point, in the middle of the game, I would do something that was very nontraditional in our games. I would call for a time out.

This was a tricky thing because no one called for a time out in the South Bronx. And after a back and forth, they would say, "What . . . ?" and I'd say, "Look, I want to do a substitution." This was unheard of! You don't do substitutions in the middle of a pick-up.

There would be lots of debate and they'd say, "Well, who do you want to put in?" And I would say, "My brother." And they would chuckle. And they would say, "Well, we see your game, so if it runs in the family, then sure, bring the guy in. What do we care?" And John would enter the game. The smirks would disappear and the chuckling would stop and invariably we would win that game.

In the middle of my sophomore year, my brother John died.

There were many times in my life when I have been facing crises and complex problems trying to fight for the good where I have seen the smirks. I have heard the chuckles of folks who say it can't be done; it will never happen. And I wish I could call for a time out. I just wish I could call for a time out and bring some hero, some heroine, in to save the day.

Growing up as a child, I was a big comic book reader and *Superman* was one of my favorites. I knew there was a force for good that was coming in to rescue all the little boys and girls from violence and injustice, and I always assumed that force was going to be Superman. Then my mother told me that Superman wasn't real. I was about eight. My mother declared, "No, no, no. There's no Superman." I started crying because I really thought Superman was coming to save us from the chaos, the violence, the danger. But no hero was coming. Realizing that nobody was coming was one of the most shocking things I learned as a young child.

I have another fantasy. That one day, not far from now, my team will be doing battle with the forces of darkness. They will be trying to reverse our progress and hurt our children, to kill their souls. And it will suddenly hit me that I can do no more because I've been in this game too long, and I have grown weary. But I won't bow my head, and I won't feel sorry for myself. I will know suddenly my time has passed and I can do no more. The forces that are arrayed against us are too powerful, too mighty. Defeat is at hand, but I will not be afraid, no, I won't bow my head. I'll look at my team and say one last time, "Let's go down fighting."

And suddenly from behind me I will hear a mighty roar and there will be the kind of sight that makes your heart sing: a group of warriors, stronger, smarter, braver. And they will come charging down to meet the enemy, and I will move to the back and look at my team and say, "Who are those heroes?" And as the battle is joined and I realize all we have fought for will not be lost, I will grab a few of those young warriors for justice and say, "Who are you? Where did you come from?" Then they will say to me, "Don't you know us? We are the next generation to take up this fight." And I'll know that my time has passed and better men and women than me will continue our struggle.

Chapter Twenty-four

●

The Call

I got the call at the worst time—not that any time for this kind of call is good, or one time is better than another. But this time the call came right in the middle of the Knicks and Chicago basketball championship series, in the spring of 1994. I am a serious Knicks fan and I was looking forward to catching the game that evening. I was in a good mood because I had been able to teach my martial arts class that night. In the past I'd never missed teaching a class, but these days it seemed I was working more and more evenings, and I often had to leave the teaching of the class to my black belt students. Not that they aren't more than capable, but I'd been missing my students, some of whom I have been with for more than ten years and are like a second family.

Class had gone well and I couldn't help but marvel at the grace and power of these young men and women as they went through their drills. I was harsher than usual on them as they practiced, correcting even the most minor misalignment of an arm or foot. I'm a tough teacher, but my students know that I love them. For many of them I am the only man in their life, and I know that I must assume the role of the stern, loving, powerful father figure. And if you knew me you would know that this suits me just fine, for it is through this role that I teach the values and discipline that I hope will keep these young people alive.

When I arrived home I threw my bag containing my martial arts gear in the corner, kissed Yvonne, said hello to Joanne, pushed the play button on the answering machine, and turned on the television. I did all of these things within fifteen seconds, as the game had already started. Yvonne and Joanne knew this was a big evening for me. That the Knicks were on and I was home in time to see them was almost a miracle, so my family forgave my poor manners.

Yvonne and I have lived together for many years, and one of the many things we have in common is having survived growing up poor in New York City. Yvonne grew up in Harlem as one of four children. She and her sister are the only ones left. Both of her brothers died before they were thirty. My family fared somewhat better, with three out of four of us still alive. My brother John died at the age of twenty-two. Joanne is Yvonne's niece; she came to live with us after her grandmother could no longer provide for her.

I paid no attention to the phone when it rang, and Yvonne answered it. It was something in her voice as she said, "All right, I'll be right there," that made me glance away from the television and pay closer attention. There was little emotion in her voice as she said, "They shot Alex." I just looked at her, the words not quite sinking in. She sounded as if she had been expecting this call for years.

"They shot Alex." And she began to get dressed to go to the emergency room, nothing more, nothing less. Right at that moment something exciting happened in the game and I found my eyes drawn to the cheering of the crowd on the television. There was something quite surreal about the moment. I looked at her again. She was proceeding mechanically, putting on one shoe, then the other while the fans were cheering some great athletic move, and my brain was still trying to comprehend.

Alex was Yvonne's nephew. At twenty-eight he was the oldest male relative she had who was still alive. His wife and Yvonne were best friends, so I had come to know Alex and his wife and son well. We only visited two or three times a year, but he was the closest thing I had to family in Harlem.

Alex's favorite hangout was on Eighth Avenue and 121st Street, where he and Yvonne had grown up. Yvonne's mother and grandmother still lived in a tenement building in that neighborhood and so I was often in that area with her to visit with her family. Yvonne said that Alex had been shot on the corner of Seventh Avenue and 121st Street and that they had taken him to Saint Luke's Hospital in Harlem.

I quickly began to prepare to drive over to pick up Yvonne's mother, who insisted on going with us to the emergency room. I wanted to put on a jacket and tie, thinking I might get answers from the nurses and doctors faster in that outfit as opposed to the jogging suit I was wearing. But Yvonne was insistent on leaving right away, so I made do with what I had on. Yvonne's comment as we left our apartment was basic: "God, please don't let him be dead." The drive to Saint Luke's from my apartment is a short one, but it seemed like one of the longest drives of my life. We picked up Yvonne's mother on Eighth Avenue, and she said, bursting into tears, that the word on the street was that Alex was dead.

I will never forget the look on Yvonne's face when her mother said that. It was a look of such heart-wrenching pain that it was all I could do to keep driving the car and not pull over to console her. I in my usual way tried to be analytical. I felt that in this case we had reason to be optimistic; rumors in Harlem are incessant and there was no reason I could see to believe that anyone really knew Alex's status. I began to recount the facts that we'd been told, reminding everybody that even this information could be wrong. "Alex was shot one time; he was hit in the body and not the head. The human body is remarkably strong, and you can survive a single gunshot wound if it doesn't do severe damage to a major organ and if help arrives quickly. Alex is in great shape. He's a big, healthy man. There's no reason we should jump to any conclusion that he's dead. Let's all calm down and wait to get to the emergency room. The odds are in our favor." My words did little to relieve the feeling of impending doom in the car.

When we arrived at the emergency room we were met on the street by Alex's wife. She was distraught and in tears. I immediately examined the look of the two young men who were with her—there I would find the truth, no matter how grim. Young men in Harlem know death. Most have had death's shadow fall over their lives and the lives of their loved ones many times. And I saw that death was in their slow walk, in the way their feet sort of kicked at an imaginary paper bag on the street. In the way their heads hung down, out of respect for the dead; the way their faces and whole bodies "took it like a man." Death.

As we got out of the car the women began to embrace one another and sob. The two men walked slowly over to me and I saw the look in the eye, the half-frown, the almost imperceptible shake of the head—no. All as if to say, "Let the women have a few more minutes of hope; we men have no illusion concerning the suddenness and finality of death. We have no hope of stalling death. We die every day and every night."

"He's gone," was all that one of them said to me, quietly and off to one side. I went to Yvonne and gave her the sad news. Then and there began the sad flood of tears from so many who knew Alex, one that seemed to last forever.

We spent the next two hours in the emergency room waiting for a doctor to come and break the news to Alex's wife. Later we waited for a chance to see the body before we left him to others. Those hours in the emergency room are a blur of crying women, men on beds in the hallways, their bodies in various states of needing repair—bandages, cursing, blood, and confusion. I was asked to identify Alex's body, and all I could think about as I saw how perfect Alex looked, handsome and powerful even in death, was that all over America young men were lying on stretchers, in hallways, on street corners, in homes, dead. Perfect in every other way, but dead.

Over the course of the next couple of days we were able to pin down the basic facts. Alex had been eating dinner in a local restaurant and went out to use a pay phone. On his way he met another young man he knew from the neighborhood. He stopped to talk. A car pulled up. A man got out with a gun. He motioned for Alex to get away and began to shoot the man Alex had just been talking to. He shot him over and over again, mostly in the head. That young man died instantly. One bullet missed its target and found Alex. He was shot through the lungs. The bullet tore a major artery; Alex's lungs filled with blood, and, unable to breathe, he died on the street in Harlem. Another innocent bystander killed.

The next few days were most difficult for me. I couldn't shake the feeling that death is always too close in Harlem. Alex had been killed where I had passed many a day and night. My staff worked in that area and they walked the same streets all the time. I thought about leaving Harlem. I have no martyr complex, and while I would love to think I would give my life for the right cause—those noble causes that we all would love to believe we might die for: freedom, equality, civil rights—I don't want to be killed just because I walked up the wrong block at the wrong time. For the first time in a long time I was afraid. How ironic to have figured a way to get out of the South Bronx, a way to find the peace that was so elusive to me as a child, only to be right back at the same place thirty years later.

And as I walked the streets of Harlem over the next couple of days and saw the children playing and laughing I had the same urge I'd had when they robbed my brother Daniel when we first moved onto Union Avenue. I wanted to yell to the children, "Get off the street! Don't you know it's not safe here? People are being killed every day. Go inside and lock your doors, stay away from your windows because you never know when a stray bullet will come flying in. Run and hide! Run and hide!"

In the end I decided to stay a little longer. The children have nowhere to go. Their families have no money to move, they have no place else to play, and it's not their fault, anyway—it's ours. We're going to have to change things so that they can play in peace and not worry about dying on the street.

Chapter Twenty-five

•

Hope in Heroes

It's a Wednesday night in October and I can't believe I've gotten away in time to be early for my martial arts class. In October and February I let new students into my classes and this class is full of them. I walk into the brightly lit gym and all eyes turn toward me. I'm walking with purpose, quickly and silently. A little boy begins to run over to me and an older student grabs his arm. I see him whispering in the younger boy's ear. I'm sure he's telling him, "You can't talk to him before class." And he's right. I talk to no one when I first come in to teach. One boy runs over and bows quickly and runs away. I nod my head in acknowledgment and continue my march to the tiny office that serves as my dressing room. I know that by now the word is out to all of the students that I'm teaching the class tonight.

In the silence of my dressing room I begin to change into my uniform, and I try to quiet my mind. It's harder than usual. The city is cutting youth services again. Our center will be affected. This very night, the center will be closed unless I can raise the money privately to keep it open. That means more running around, more late nights, more lost weekends. That doesn't bother me, but it causes me to miss my classes. For decades I have taught martial arts in this school. For many of those years I hardly ever missed a class. Now I'm lucky if I can make it one night a week. My three black belt students are good teachers, but they're young and still need my guidance.

I dress, leave the room, and go back into the gym. If you saw me now you might think I'm stern, even mean. No smile is on my face. I scan the room looking for any sign that my students are fooling around and not warming up the way they are supposed to. As my gaze travels around the room students stop playing tag and laughing and joking, and pretend that they're stretching or practicing their kicks. They hope I haven't seen them playing around, that they have fooled me. I pretend they have. I turn my back on them and silently go through my own drills, letting the tension and drama build. And suddenly I clap my hands two times and fifty children are dashing every which way trying to get in line. The older students have been waiting for this moment and know where to go, the younger students dart around trying to find an empty place in line. For a few moments it looks like everyone is playing a game of musical chairs.

I stand in front of them, looking unhappy and displeased. Everyone wonders who is out of place or not standing up straight. This is part of my act. Finally I begin the class and then I'm lost in the teaching. I'm trying to bring magic into the lives of these kids. To bring a sense of wonder and amazement. I can feel the students losing themselves and focusing on me. They are finally mine. I have them all to myself. I have crowded all the bad things out of their minds. The test they failed, the father who won't come by to see them, the dinner that won't be on the stove when they get home. I've pushed it all away by force of will and magic.

This is my time and I know all the tricks. I yell, I scream, I fly through the air with the greatest of ease. I take my black belt students and I slam them on the floor and they pop up like those weighted Weebles dolls that can't stay down. I throw them through the air as if they were feathers, and they land and roll and are back up unhurt and unafraid. The new students can't believe their eyes. And they begin to believe in magic again.

And by the time the class is ending their eyes are wide with amazement and respect, and they look at me differently. And I line them up and I talk to them. I talk to them about values, about violence, about hope. I try to build within each one a reservoir of strength that they can draw from as they face the countless tribulations, small and large, that poor children face every day. And I try to convince each one that I know their true value, their worth as human beings, their special gift that God gave to them. And I hope they will make it to the next class with something left in that reservoir for me to add to week by week. It is from that reservoir that they will draw the strength to resist the drugs, the guns, the violence.

When class ends I dress, and now things are different. I speak to every-one. Students come up to shake hands and we bow in greeting. I am back to being Geoff to them, their friend. As a group of us walk up 108th Street together I scan the street for signs of danger. This, after all, is a neighbor-hood where more than ten adolescents have been killed by guns this year alone. I call one of the youngest students over to me. He is only five and comes to class with his older brother. I see that his jacket is open and I stoop down to zip it up.

The jacket is old and beat-up, probably belonged to his brother last year. The zipper is broken. He believes I can fix it. Why not? After watching me in class he believes that I can do anything. His face is filled with anticipa-tion. It's cold outside and the long blocks he has to walk in the cold will seem shorter if I fix his jacket. I try to fix the zipper. I can't. Instead, I show him how to use one hand to hold his jacket closed close around his neck. I readjust his hand several times so he understands that there is a certain way to do it that meets with my approval. This is also part of the act—all of the attention to detail keeps him from feeling ashamed. I notice his nose is running and take out the package of tissues that I keep in my pocket for just this purpose and wipe his nose. He doesn't object like most five-year-olds. He loves the care and concern. As I watch him cross the street with his brothers and friends, holding his jacket closed with his hand, the spell is broken for me. No more magic. Just little five-year-olds in raggedy jackets that won't close, trying to stay warm on a cold night. I scribble a note to myself to remember to find a way to get some jackets. Winter is coming.

My two black belts usually walk with me after class and stay with me until I catch a cab. I tell them it's not necessary, but they are there to make sure I get home all right. What a world. So dangerous that children feel that a third-degree black belt needs an escort to get home safely. The sad thing is, with all the guns and drugs in this community, they know I'm no safer than anyone else.

This community, like many across this country, is not safe for children, and they usually walk home at night filled with fear and apprehension. But when I walk with them after class they are carefree, like children ought to be. They have no fear. They believe that if anything happens they'll be safe because I'm there. I'll fly through the air and with my magic karate I'll dispatch whatever evil threatens them.

Today, when the young people of the Harlem Children's Zone see me standing on the corner, watching them walk into their buildings, they believe what children used to believe, that there are adults who can protect them. And because of that belief they see me as larger than life, like Superman or Batman. And I let them believe this, even if my older black belts and I know different. Because in a world that is so cold and so harsh, children need heroes. Heroes give hope, and if these children have no hope they will have no future. And so I play the role of hero for them, even if I have to resort to cheap tricks and theatrics.

And if I could get the mayors, and the governors, and the president to look into the eyes of the five-year-olds of this nation, dressed in old raggedy clothes, whose zippers are broken but whose dreams are still alive, they would know what I know—that children need people to fight for them. To stand with them on the most dangerous streets, in the dirtiest hallways, in their darkest hours. We as a country have been too willing to take from our weakest when times get hard. People who allow this to happen must be educated, must be challenged, must be turned around.

If we are to save our children then we must become people they will look up to. Children need heroes now more than ever because the poor children of this nation live with monsters every day. Monsters deprive them of heat in the winter; they don't fix their sinks and toilets; they let garbage pile up in their hallways; they kick them out of their homes; they beat them, shoot them, stab them—sometimes to death—they rape their bodies and their minds. Sometimes they lurk under the stairs. They scuttle around in the dark; you hear them in the walls gnawing, squeaking, occasionally biting a little finger.

We have failed our children. They live in a world where danger lurks all around them and their playgrounds are filled with broken glass, crack vials, and sudden death. And the stuff of our nightmares when we were children is the common reality for children today. Monsters are out there and claiming children in record numbers. And so we must stand up and be visible heroes, fighting for our children. I want people to understand the crisis that our children face, and I want people to act.

Geoffrey Canada is the president and CEO of the Harlem Children's Zone, a nonprofit, community-based organization that President Barack Obama called "an all-encompassing, all-hands-on-deck anti-poverty effort that is literally saving a generation of children" and the *New York Times Magazine* deemed "one of the most ambitious social experiments of our time." Canada has become nationally recognized for his pioneering work and as a passionate advocate for education reform. Jonathan Kozol called him "one of the few authentic heroes of New York and one of the best friends children have, or ever will have, in our nation," and Oprah Winfrey simply refers to him as "an angel from God." He is a graduate of Bowdoin College and the Harvard School of Education, and is the recipient of honorary degrees from Harvard University, Bowdoin College, Williams College, John Jay College, Bank Street College, and Meadville Lombard Theological Seminary. Canada's work has been profiled on *60 Minutes, Good Morning America,* and *The Colbert Report,* as well as in articles for the *Wall Street Journal, Washington Post,* and many more publications. He is featured in Davis Guggenheim's documentary *Waiting for "Superman"*. A sixth-degree black belt, Canada is also the founder of the Chang Moo Kwan Martial Arts School, where he continues to teach violence-prevention methods and the principles of tae kwon do.